The
Africana
Worship Book

The Africana Worship Book

Year A

General Editor, Valerie Bridgeman Davis, PhD

Associate Editor, Safiyah Fosua

DISCIPLESHIP RESOURCES

PO BOX 340003 • NASHVILLE, TN 37203-0003
www.discipleshipresources.org

Cover design by Robert Mott.
Interior design by PerfecType, Nashville, TN.

ISBN 13: 978-088177-490-0
ISBN 10: 0-88177-490-1

Library of Congress Control Number 2006932056

For information regarding rights and permissions, contact Discipleship Resources, PO Box 340003, Nashville TN 37203-0003; fax 615-340-1789.

What Others Are Saying about
The Africana Worship Book

Worship is the lifeblood of the church and the African American worshipping community in particular! Now we finally have *The Africana Worship Book* as a useful tool in planning worship in our Black tradition! It speaks to our culture, our vitality, and our history as we worship the God who brought us from a mighty long way! This worship planning book is exceptional! Well written and researched! It reminds us what my mentor Dr. Zan Holmes, Jr. taught me years ago, "It's all right to be black and United Methodist at the same time!" Thank you for giving us such a useful resource!

–Tyrone D. Gordon, Senior Pastor, St. Luke "Community" United Methodist Church
Dallas, Texas

The Africana Worship Book reverberates with "God's heartbeat and the heartbeat of the gathered people." It is a resource that satisfies my longing for relevant, prophetic, and "keeping it real" God-talk. Dr. Valerie Bridgeman Davis and Dr. Safiyah Fosua offer creative prayers, meditations, and choral reading collections that invite us to bring our whole lives, our yearnings and shortcomings, into the worship experience, I was stunned by the power and forthright liturgical honesty of this book. As people of the Word, the Spirit, and ancestral legacies spoken and implicit, we sometimes find ourselves bereft and numb when the incongruity and surprise of our twenty-first century lives collide with what we know about who we are in the sight of God. These resources remind me that as a people of faith, we are still on the journey toward a hopeful future.

–Barbara Holmes
Dean, Memphis Theological Seminary

There are times when the written word assists us to experience the presence and movement of God's spirit. Reading the heart and soul-felt expressions of worship in *The Africana Worship Book* provides that experience of God over and over again.

In words that speak truth to our hearts, the petitions, confessions, and joys of our souls are reflected in these pages. Thanks be to God for those who emptied themselves so that the fullness of God could be revealed.

–Bishop Linda Lee
Wisconsin Area of The United Methodist Church

This collection of resources for Africana worship fills a void too long occupied by dependence on materials from other cultures. Keyed to the lectionary year, these liturgical elements nevertheless reflect appropriately and creatively the spirituality of the Black Church today.

–Dr. Ella Mitchell
Visiting Professor at Interdenominational Theological Center in Atlanta

I have been blessed by *The Africana Worship Book*. As an African serving in the African American ministry context, I believe this resource has been the missing link to dynamic and culturally relevant liturgy for congregations in the African Diaspora. It provides a significant liturgical bridge to *Songs of Zion*, *The Faith We Sing* and *The United Methodist Hymnal*. It's an exciting beginning, and will unleash the creativity of many who are serious about doing and being the Church of Jesus Christ "for such a time as this." The richness and quality of the congregational prayers, meditations, choral readings, etc. contained in this resource celebrate a different approach to worship resourcing that has been dormant for too long. *The Africana Worship Book* will be a true gift to the general church and society that accurately represents the ethos and pathos of the liturgical, spiritual and social experience of God's children within the African Diaspora.

–Rev. Kelvin Sauls

Contents

Contributors

About the General Editor: **Rev. Dr. Valerie Bridgeman Davis, Ph.D.,** Biblical Studies (Hebrew Bible), teaches Old Testament and preaching and worship at Memphis Theological Seminary. She directs the Return Beat: Syncopating the Arts and Theology Institute at the seminary. A poet and liturgical dancer, Dr. Bridgeman Davis is a consultant for the 21st Century Africana Worship Resource Project.

About the Associate Editor: **Rev. Dr. Safiyah Fosua** is the Director of Invitational Preaching Ministries at the General Board of Discipleship in Nashville, TN and a clergy member of the Greater New Jersey Annual Conference. Dr. Fosua writes resources for the preaching section of the General Board of Discipleship Worship Website (www.umcworship.org).

Rev. Dr. Eugene Blair is a clergy member of the Detroit Annual Conference, where he serves as the Director of the Office of African American Spiritual Formation. Dr. Blair is a former Dean of The Upper Room Chapel.

Carolyn W. Dandridge serves as the Communications Coordinator at the General Board of Discipleship in Nashville, Tennessee. Carolyn Dandridge and Catrinia Harrison are mother and daughter.

Rev. Joseph W. Daniels, Jr. is the Senior Pastor of Emory United Methodist Church in Washington, D.C.

Rev. Junius Dotson is the Senior Pastor of Saint Mark United Methodist Church, in Wichita, Kansas.

Catrinia N. Harrison is a member of the Faith A.M.E. Zion Church in Baton Rouge, Louisiana, and is a senior at Southern University, majoring in Child Psychology. Catrinia's "Deliverance" was written when she was sixteen years old.

Rev. Sherrie Dobbs Johnson is the pastor of Grace United Methodist Church in Brooklyn, New York.

Rev. Dr. Kwasi I. Kena is the Director of Evangelism Ministries at the General Board of Discipleship in Nashville, TN and a clergy member of the Greater New Jersey Annual Conference. Dr. Kena writes resources for the GBOD Evangelism website (http://www.gbod.org/evangelism/).

Toni Payne is a Systems Support Administrator for the General Board of Discipleship.

Tony Peterson is a New Solutions Project Manager at the General Board of Discipleship in Nashville, Tennessee.

Ciona D. Rouse is a freelance writer for United Methodist News Service and a former staff member of the General Board of Discipleship, Nashville, TN.

The **Rev. Lillian C. Smith** is the Associate General Secretary for the Division on Ministries with Young People at the General Board of Discipleship in Nashville, Tennessee

Rev. Marilyn E. Thornton is the Development Editor of African American Resources at The United Methodist Publishing House and the Director of Christian Education at South End UMC in Nashville, TN.

Rev. Tim Warner serves as the pastor of the St. Mark's United Methodist Church of Boyd, Maryland and is a member of the Baltimore-Washington Annual Conference of the United Methodist Church.

Rev. Stacey Cole Wilson serves as the Associate Pastor of Linthicum Heights UMC in Linthicum Heights, Maryland, and is a member of the Baltimore-Washington Annual Conference of The United Methodist Church.

Foreword

"Lord, How Come We Here?"

For insight on the meaning of worship and spirituality from an Africana perspective, we pose the question, **"Lord, how come we here?"** It is a simple question in the idiom of the people who first raised it that way. I believe this question can be spoken again in this way–even in the twenty-first century–for two reasons: (1) because God speaks to our human experience and not to our affectations, and (2) because the profound expressions of African people, and in particular, African American people who raised it in this profound, grammatical way, were shaped in a terrible time of uprootedness and transition.

They raised this question as the Africans' first encounter with God in America came, when they were struggling to bridge the communication gap and the cultural gap between themselves and their captors. The language patterns they developed were a hybrid of their native language(s) and that of the host society. Just as the host language was imperfectly understood, so was the Africans' sense of being and purpose confused by their arrival in a new and alien land.

How come we here? was a very logical question for the Africans to raise in this new setting: forcibly torn from their homeland and the routine of their settled lives in their own villages and towns without their consent; herded on death ships like cattle to come to America to be slaves to their capriciously cruel captors; auctioned off in the marketplace –not even as human beings–but mere property to be bought, owned and used; stripped of every vestige of their dignity and respectability; kin separated from kin, tribe separated from tribe, sons and daughters separated from mothers and fathers, and all separated from the place of spiritual and human meaning in their lives. In this strange land to which they were brought to bear these unusual and heavy burdens, the spiritual strivings and wrestlings began; i.e., the soul's inquiry into the worth, meaning and purpose of their lives. **"Lord, how come we here?"** is asked in an effort to bridge the communication gap. The spiritual implications of the question are vast indeed.

The spiritual strivings of these transplanted Africans began long before, and continued long after, the so-called "Magnolia Missions" of white Christians converted them to Christianity and had a chance to plant the heretical notion that these Africans had no identity and were cursed and ordained by God to be but "hewers of wood" and "drawers of water." Even though they were stripped of everything of their former lives and left with nothing else of their prior selves but a mere gossamer of their spiritual identity, these involuntarily depersonalized expatriate souls used this last fragile fiber of faith–half-forgotten and therefore half-remembered–to ponder the most piercingly profound and perennial of spiritual questions: **"Lord, how come we here?"**

The spiritual implications of the question would take on ever-increasing significance as the developing African American experience unfolded in the complex, diverse, and human relationships that make that experience unique. Clearly, the question: **how come we here?** is much easier to explain than it is to answer. That requires the complete acceptance of God's inscrutable agenda, by faith alone. The obvious answer is that we are here because God has chosen to bring us here. But it is the "why" behind the divine choice that we truly long to understand. We know by faith that in the Divine Scheme "all things work together for good," but what we do not know, and cannot know, is, "all things." We see through a glass darkly and perhaps dimly, and that is because we are mortal and our vision is limited. We will see more clearly when our vision is improved by a level of faith we have not yet achieved.

In the meantime, life has to be lived and confronted on a daily basis, for survival itself is the first condition of "survival-for-what?" If we are not here when the glass is cleared and the revelation is made, then we will never know **"how come we here?"**

In their struggle with the "in the meantime," African Americans have made an effort to deal with this spiritual question and to appropriate the meaning of suffering and their experience of pain with expressions of soulful soliloquies, songs, sayings, sermons, and shouts; but also dances, confessions, poems, raps, and other forms of spiritual responses. All are a part of the "stuff" that forms and informs African American spirituality. All are a part of what my late teacher Howard Thurman at Boston University used to call their "life's working paper." For, in a real sense, it is made up of the creative combination of what a people are in their many and various parts and how they react to the process of living. There are the personal and deep longings of every African American (even among those who act it out in rage and strange and utterly destructive behavior) to be simply viewed and received just like everybody else, as who they are, and to be free to be themselves on their own terms: just "one of God's children" with strengths and weaknesses, gifts and limitations, and all of the rest of the characteristics common to the human lot. And, yet again, African Americans are tied to others who share a common heritage, history and hope, and who look like themselves—sing and shout, pray and die—even though sometimes in a different mien.

 In its many facets and in so many different ways, African American spirituality as expressed in worship identifies its suffering with Moses and the Hebrew children, and their struggle and suffering, and the Hebrews who insisted that any Pharaoh who holds the children in bondage must let God's people go by whatever means the Lord chooses! For as so many faithful African Americans put it, "You are God *all by yourself!*" This means that even if God has to roll back the waters of the Red Sea and drown Pharaoh's army, or cause "Jordan to stand still," God's children have to get to the Promised Land of freedom. At the heart of any form of African American spirituality that is true to its Africana roots and a Wesleyan heritage is the unquestionable, uncontestable, undebateable, orthodox, and dogmatic belief that the act of the liberating of God's people is an amazing act of divine grace.

It would be unfair and untrue to simply paint the picture of Africana worship and African American spirituality, or the worship and spirituality of any people, as only a life of struggle and merely a response to suffering. There is always within its very fiber a fierce and abiding sense of justice and what is right, and a response to the active presence of **grace**, and even **"grace upon grace,"** (especially among Wesleyans and Methodists of whatever stripe),[1] as they ponder the question, **"Lord, how come we here?"** In doing so, they incorporate into their struggle for meaning the notions of justice, freedom, and love.

---

[1] See William B. McClain, *Black People in The Methodist Church: Whither Thou Goest* (Nashville: Abingdon Press, 1984), for a discussion of Wesleyan groups, the theology, and their common history and heritage, especially pp. 15ff. See also Grant S. Shockley, *Heritage and Hope: The African American Presence in United Methodism* (Nashville: Abingdon Press, 1991).

African American spirituality is also a response to God's act of grace. We hear it in the classical and traditional prayer of the old-fashioned steward (an office still maintained in the Black denominational Methodist churches, and even in some African American United Methodist Churches. When I served as pastor of Union United Methodist Church in Boston for ten years, that church continued the tradition of the office of steward, even when the national church had abandoned it.) As I tried to point out in an earlier work I wrote, *Come Sunday: The Liturgy of Zion*, it does not matter at all that this same prayer was prayed last Sunday or Wednesday night at prayer meeting or at any number of other worship settings. It is still the African American response to grace and one of the answers to the spiritual question: **"Lord, how come we here?"**

In the words of one of the stewards or one of the other prayer warriors as they come before the throne of grace, knee-bowed and body bent:

> "We thank you that you watched over us all night
> long while we slumbered and slept in the very image
> of death. Early this morning you touched us with the
> fingertip of love . . . I want to thank you that when I
> rose this morning, my bed was not my cooling board
> and my sheet was not my winding cloth. Through
> your goodness and mercy you have seen fit to leave
> us here to pick and choose our own praying ground.
> We thank you for protecting us from dangers, seen
> and unseen. We thank you for leading us from one
> good degree of grace to another . . ." [2]

Human survival seems to be threatened by the hour. The struggle to be witnesses and to participate in God's plan for the coming of the Kingdom cannot be separated from the struggle to survive our cultural holocaust. Spirituality as expressed in worship is the glue that connects the two struggles. In an age of rage, it is a counsel of reconciliation; in an age of hostility, it promotes healing; as we struggle with evil and imperfection, it encourages us to appreciate and glorify what is positive and good. It reminds us that there is good in all of us because there is God in

---

[2] Excerpt from *Come Sunday: The Liturgy of Zion* by William McClain (c) 1990 by Abingdon Press Used by permission. See also Frederick Hilborn Talbot, *African American Worship: New Eyes for Seeing* (Lima, Ohio: Fairway Press, 1998, pp. 72-73 for a version of this prayer heard in the A.M.E. Church. There are many variations on this classical African American prayer with denominational, regional, and doctrinal nuances and emphases, e.g., whether it is a Deacon in Baptist circles or stewards and others in Wesleyan and various African American churches.

each of us. When the world beats us down, dismisses us as worthless, calls us everything else but a child of God, Africana spirituality reminds us that we are a chosen people, chosen for a task not yet fully revealed, but we can wait on the Lord, patiently and faithfully, until our time comes. It reminds us that we must be ready when God is ready. That's why we are here and why we can celebrate God's gracious gifts to us, and that is why we are rejoicing that we are here.

We hear the African American response to the experience of grace as the people gather, whether there be two or three, or two or three thousands, singing and praising God and shouting about "Your grace and mercy brought me through, living each moment all because of you. I want to thank you and praise you, too. Your grace and mercy brought me through." Some quietly, with reverence in their hearts and thanksgiving within the very depths of their grateful souls, give thanks for this miraculous pouring out of this matchless, unfathomable, unspeakable and amazing grace. Others may even quietly wipe away the tears of joy. It is their own response to the question, **"Lord, how come we here?"** But some of the people cannot be quiet, nor can they be still. They can contain themselves no longer. To avoid the "rocks crying out" in response to the presence, reality, and manifestation of God's overwhelming grace, they shout and scream out as if their whole selves—mind, soul, spirit, and body—have been taken over, possessed by an unseen controlling force beyond the ability of any human eyes to perceive. Their responses are passionate, and their emotional outpourings are often tears of joy, praise and thanksgiving, sometimes unintelligible as if it came from another world, and some even dance between the pews and in the aisles. Their uncontrollable screams, shouts and chants begin decipherably and crystal clear: "Hallelujah! Thank you, Jesus! Praise the Lord! Hallelujah!" Not everyone, but some said, **"Lord, that is how come we are here!"**

So, in a real sense, and in a Wesleyan perspective with Africana roots and Methodist identity, African American spirituality is a response to the reality of suffering, as well as a response to the experience of grace. This effort in *The Africana Worship Book* on the part of these writers is another way of helping us respond to suffering and grace in a Wesleyan key. The faithful and able authors of these worship helps in poems and prayers, litanies and meditations, invitations to discipleship, creedal statements, and many other useful worship aids have tried to help us continue to respond to the question: **"Lord, how come we here?"**

Several of them are former students of mine, some in the Wesley Theological Seminary regular Master's programs, others in doctoral programs, and still others in programs or settings where I have had the privilege and honor, by God's grace, to be their teacher and mentor. I commend them for work well done, and I commend and recommend their offerings as wonderful gifts to help the *whole* church respond to the experience of God's grace. Indeed, that is what true worship is: to remember where we have known God's grace, even in the midst of persecution, suffering, trials, and all manner of injustice, to be challenged to face the present with faith and courage, and to have hope about the future. That is what true worship is: for the people of God to gather around the Word and the sacrament and to stand in the present with one hand grasping the past and the other reaching toward the future.

The truth is, the question from Africana **"Lord, how come we here?",** is really a question for all worshipers to raise in whatever denomination, or whatever region of the world, or whatever culture, or whatever ethnic group, as they come into God's sanctuary. Or, in the words of the General Editor of this book, Dr. Valerie Bridgeman Davis: as hearts are "open to the flame of God's presence in the Spirit," we might ask afresh the question, and with all of our twenty-first century sophistication in communications and technology, **"Lord, how come we here?"**

William B. McClain
Mary Elizabeth Joyce Professor of Preaching and Worship
Wesley Theological Seminary
Washington, D.C.

An Introduction

Africana Worship in the Twenty-First Century

> "When God is present, we respond in body and in spirit. Sometimes the eye swells, other times the feet leap, but inevitably the heart journeys home,"–Dr. Barbara A. Holmes, *Joy Unspeakable: Contemplative Practices of the African American Church* (Augsburg Fortress: Minneapolis, 2004) p. 52.

Worship is response. Worship recognizes that God is present, or at least recognizes that God might, in the vernacular of some African American church people, "show up and show out." Worship is human response to the Mystery of all Worlds. It is an expression of the divine reflected back by the creature to that divinity. Worship allows people to use their embodied selves in an authentic way that honors humanity and revels in God. This worship of which I speak may happen in the kitchen or the cathedral with equal abandon and awe; it may occur at the altar or the arts museum when awe of something and/or someone larger consumes us. We worship.

This phrase "show up and show out" presumes an active God who wants to be in companionship and communication with God's people. Such response, as Barbara A. Holmes notes, is evident in swaying bodies and tapping feet, in weeping eyes and prayerful hearts. Worship leads our hearts homeward to God, who created and continues to form us.

When I was invited to serve as consultant for the 21st Century Africana Worship Project, I was glad to come on. What excited me about the project was twofold: one, the project would give me an opportunity to test my own theories about worship and planning a worship experience; and two, the project would give me an opportunity to practice the discipline of the Christian liturgical year, since the project created "real time" resources by people of African descent for the whole church. The following spring, I served as a keynote speaker and the final preacher for a "This Holy Mystery" Conference in Nashville, a conference designed to ignite afresh a passion of weekly serving and receiving of the Lord's Supper in the larger church.

In both these events, the overwhelming issue was whether what the church has historically said and done in creeds, in prayers, and in the ways it arranged its worship could and does speak to the present and coming generations. I am convinced that if historic worship doesn't speak to the present generation, it can. Corporate worship gathers people together to praise and petition God, to reverence and to revel in God. This worship gives credence to God's majestic otherness and God's very nearness to us, God's incarnational gift of God's self. So we gather to hear from and to speak to God. These qualities of worship were true for first-century seekers, and they are just as true for twenty-first century saints.

In a world that is increasingly smaller because we can connect via news and Internet in seconds, we experience the world sometimes as despairingly large. In the world of broadband connections, instant messages, and text messaging, we often come to worship and experience alienation rather than community.

New forms of worship and thinking about worship are emerging to help address a sense of alienation. The most notable among them is the "emerging" church phenomenon. If one looks closely enough, "emerging church" seems suspiciously like 1960s "Jesus People" meet technology and sound bites. Or, it looks like first century house-church intimacy meets mass gatherings with the same goals for intimate, personal, small group interactions in the crowd. In any event, these emerging congregations give voice to a longing of worshipers to navigate their own concerns, and to comprehend the heart of God.

How must we help worshipers navigate their concerns and God's heart? There are principles that must guide every expression of worship. The following list is not exhaustive, or even extensive, but I do believe the points on it are essential.

First, is the worship relevant? I do not mean by relevant that the worship is personally satisfying to a particular set of worshipers, but rather that the worship meets the criterion of conversation between the culture and the Covenant (the biblical record), and that the volume is "up" on the biblical side of that equation and given weightier consideration. Worship that caters to personal preferences not tempered by Christ runs the risk of being accepted, but not transformative.

Second, is the worship theocentric/Christocentric? There are several lenses through which to view the world; if the church, however, believes that God was in Christ reconciling the world to God's own self, then our singing, our praying, our drama, our dancing, our preaching must hold as a central underpinning the Christ event, with the hum of the birth, life, death, and resurrection of Jesus raising a joyful refrain. Christian worship, even "good-news-got-to-tell-it" worship, must always push us beyond human narcissism. It must open a way, a clearing to the presence of God.

Since I believe that worship opens an aperture to the presence of God, I believe every effort ought to be made to sharpen the focus of a worship experience. We gather to offer thanks for what God has done and praise for who God is on our collective and individual behalf. We can't plan worship; only worshipers may decide whether and how they will worship. The best that leaders may do is plan an experience that gives the radical nature of God's love, the gospel, the best hearing for the people gathered that day. Such planning of an experience comes with a default prayerful attitude, since none of us knows who will be present before that experience is planned. But this mystery of un-knowing should propel us to creatively think through what the most basic of human desires are, as well as our best and boldest theological guess of what God desires for this encounter.

Such planning takes chutzpah and faith. Such planning presumes that worship is ongoing, constant, and surprising at every turn. So, the question becomes whether we have created a space in which God is "free" to work and speak and encounter us, and us God. If the chief end of humans is to worship and glorify God, then the worship "moment" is to remind us that all life is filled with God's presence and intentions. Worship gatherings testify to the incarnational presence of God still at work in and among us; worship gatherings give voice to our need for God and for one another. In God's presence, truth and transformation kiss each other.

Worship not only opens a vantage of seeing and experiencing, but worship also must be planned participation. Much of what passes for worship has been reduced to show up, take a seat, wait for the people up front to do their thing, go home. This inactive, passive mode of worship often leads to boredom and irrelevance.

I had the privilege of leading an arts and theology institute in which students were challenged to design worship that was God-filled and God-focused, art-filled and artful; worship that was compelling and inviting. In the worship service that was designed, worship leaders led congregants in singing and chanting, choral clapping and movement prayer. They acted out the sermon; the celebrant approached the table with a child in arms for the call; planners threw pairs of shoes throughout the room for the visual effect of a journey; dancing and miming ensued after the sermon, and congregants got up and danced. The service culminated with lifting people up (literally) as a benediction to lift people up in prayer and encouragement, and finally a sung benediction. It was one of the most profound worship experiences of my own life, and person after person echoed my own response. The mixture of quiet reflection, video meditation, movement, joy, and repentance was balanced, profound, and biblically resonant. Though I am trying here to describe it, the truth is that experience is indescribable. That inability to be described is the nature of worship that taps into a divine space—our best efforts fail at reproducing that moment in word, or even in subsequent events. Our best chance is to try to become consistent at listening to both God's heartbeat and the heartbeat of the gathered people.

This volume is a culmination of that first consultation. I served as primary editor on the project. Users (and I do hope we have created work that may be used time and again and for years to come) will find themes of hope, of oppression and deliverance, of love and redemption. Users also will find celebration and lament, which we have come to believe, is celebration also. The pieces are suitable for worship bulletins, newsletters, and public and private worship. There are places where I made the editorial decision for community, e.g., pluralizing the first person language in confession (from "I" to "we"), in order to reflect the communal as well as the personal nature of confession. Sometimes, I believed the work was mislabeled. For example, a "call to confession" that was really a confessional prayer, or sometimes a work might be labeled "invocation," but really was a litany of confession.

Something seemingly so simple as whether to use "leader" and "people' or "one voice" "many voices" or "one" and "many" caused some struggle. I finally settled on One/Many, recognizing that some worshipers may have no "voice," e.g., many people who are hearing impaired. Trying to stay as close to the writers' work, I also wanted to make sure the words were as strong and as active as they could be. Worship is active, even our meditation is active reflection on God. Rarely, but sometimes, I made the editorial decision to cut where I thought the writer was trying to "force" some correlations among lectionary texts in a litany or choral reading. These decisions reflect only our commitment to a particular kind of consistency, and are not a statement about the quality of the work of the writer.

So, those who used these resources from the website will notice some marked differences in some of the work.

I had two overarching concerns for the worship: was it Wesleyan in its style and commitments; was it Africana in its sensibilities and tone? Because the work was designed to help United Methodist worshipers especially, it was important that the work reflect the concerns of sacramental living, of hearts open to the flame of God's presence in the Spirit. We also worked deliberately to be liturgical, following a style that is recognizable as a liturgical form. We wanted the worship to be traditional, contemporary, and contextual. In such a worship design, we free ourselves to come honestly before God and to hear and speak truth.

In the end, the project kept coming back to "real words," "real ritual," and "real desperation." As we wrote, we constantly asked ourselves whether we had addressed the human desperation expressed in modern living. Had we offered a God who hears and satiates our desperations and longings? To be honest, we may not have always pulled it off. But we have always tried. We have come to this work with a mission to express the heart's longing through the lenses of Africana experiences throughout the world. We have been a bit myopic and North American at times, but we have continued to search for that pulse of a people who, in the face of colonialization, slavery, displacement, and disenfranchisement, worshiped a moving and traveling God who went before, dwelled among, and came after them. These worship pieces are offerings in honor of the people and the God.

Valerie Bridgeman Davis

Twenty-One Questions to Consider for Designing Worship

Writing liturgy for the church is not a private affair. Writers and worship planners do not bring only their history and experiences to the task, but as much as possible designers and writers of worship events must try to bring the lives and histories of congregants, indeed of the Christian church since and before its inception until now. I offered the following questions to consultation participants as we sought to write with the whole church—not just the United Methodist communion of believers—in mind. These questions are not arranged in order of importance, as I believe one might start with any one of them to get to profound, grace-filled, godly worship.

1. Is the worship biblically resonated?
2. Is the worship theologically sound?
3. Is it ritually profound?
4. Is worship invitational?
5. Is this worship contextually relevant? Does worship reflect the culture(s), lands, and peoples gathered for worship?
6. Does the worship open an aperture to the presence of God? Have we created space for God to work and speak and encounter us, and us God?
7. Is the worship participatory? Or, are there simply "talking heads" up front that we may "tune out"?
8. Does worship pull people from the outer edges into the center?
9. Does worship incorporate gifts from the larger church (worldwide) into our local context?
10. Does this worship challenge our local context to be a witness of God through the holy, catholic (universal) church? Does the worship

"prophesy" a more inclusive reality than the one the congregation currently knows?

11. Did we leave appropriate space for stillness and silence?

12. Does worship incarnate God in Christ, begging participants to be reconciled to God?

13. Do the words of the liturgy bog down and drown out rhythm and mystery of the liturgy? Or, are litanies and prayers easy to enter, with refrains and rhythms that hold the central message in place? Is there a "heartbeat" (rhythm) worshippers can carry beyond this "thin line" moment?

14. Is worship hermetically sealed? Does it have one way in and one way out, and is it over when it's over, not carrying worshipers into the world to continue to praise, worship, repent, grow, and work?

15. Is worship permeable? Are there several entry points into Divine mystery and is it portable into the rest of the worshiper's life?

16. Is worship democratic? Does it allow voices from the center and the margin to commingle in such a way that there is no clear dominant voice? Have we invited the communion of saints from the beginning of the church's existence to the present day to speak? Do we have a word from the Old Testament, the New Testament, and the Now Testament? Do we believe God continues to speak?

17. Does the music we sing, pray, and dance reflect the reality of more than a "village" God? Are we creating theology by our worship that says God is truly the God of all universes, places, and times?

18. Did we use technology wisely and economically? Did we allow the "bells and whistles" to get in the way of the simplicity of grace?

19. Is worship visionary and prophetic? Does this worship service point us to God of the whole creation, God who loves diversity in color and sunsets, in temperature and foliage? In mountains and valleys, in rushing waterfall and gentle-flowing brooks?

20. Is worship sensory-rich? Does worship use art in ways that God is danced back into the consciousness of people? Do we sing God into the room? Do we vision God into the room with banners and clips? Do we act God into the room?

21. Does this worship return us to the miracle of hearing on the day of Pentecost, and to the great celebration around the throne of God when the reign of God is fully and completely realized and we out of every tongue, language, tribe, nation, gender, and age, lift our voices in awesome wonder of God who is majestic, powerful, holy, generous, friend, glorious, wonderful, and worthy of all this worship?

Resources for Thinking about Worship in African American Experiences

Abbington, James, ed., *Readings in African-American Church Music and Worship* (GIA Publications, 2001).

Abbington, James, ed., *Spirits that Dwell in Deep Woods: The Prayer and Praise Hymns of the Black Religious Experience* (GIA Publications, 2004).

African American Heritage Hymnal (GIA Publications, 2001).

Costen, Melva Wilson, *In Spirit and In Truth: The Music of African American Worship* (Westminster, December 2004).

Costen, Melva Wilson, *African American Christian Worship* (Abingdon, 1993).

Hall Lawrence, Beverly, *Reviving the Spirit: A Generation of African Americans Goes Home to Church* (Grover Press, 1997).

Hill, Kenneth, *Reflections on Black Worship: Expressing a Way of Prayer (Legacy Publishing,* 1998).

Holmes, Barbara A., *Joy Unspeakable: Contemplative Practices of the Black Church* (Fortress Press, 2004).

Johnson Reagon, Bernice, *If you Don't Go, Don't Hinder Me: The African American Sacred Song Tradition* (University of Nebraska Press, 2001).

Lincoln, C. Eric, *The Black Church in the African American Experience* (Duke University Press, 1990).

McClain, William B., *Come Sunday, The Liturgy of Zion* (Abingdon, 1990).

Songs of Zion (Abingdon, 1981).

Walker, Wyatt T., *Somebody's Calling My Name: Black Sacred Music and Social Change* (Judson Press, 1983).

Washington, James Melvin, Ph.D., *Conversations with God: Two Centuries of Prayers by African Americans* (San Francisco: Harper Collins Publishers, 1994).

Talbot, Frederick Hilborn, *African American Worship: New Eyes for Seeing* (Fairway Press, 1998). [out of print, being revised for republication]

Meditations for Gathering

How Many Opportunities?

(Note: the days left mentioned in the meditation may need to be modified according to the calendar.)

Three hundred sixty three: that's how many days I have left to praise God this year. I don't know how time slipped by me so quickly last year. I intended to be more thankful for all you've done, but one thing or another always came up. But this is a new year.

I have three hundred sixty three chances to reach a soul for Christ. Last year, I meant to call or write or drop by that hurting family that stayed on my mind for days. I don't know where the time goes sometimes. I guess I was so busy doing things that I rarely made a difference. But this is a new year.

I have three hundred sixty three opportunities to do something for the Lord. Maybe I should get started today. . .

(Kwasi I. Kena, Epiphany Sunday, Years A, B, C)

Epiphany
(Isaiah 60:4-6)

Nothing matches it–
Lifting your eyes from washing
Or folding clothes,
And in the distance the dust
Of tires bring back a child,
Long gone, not forgotten
Prayed for . . .

Nothing compares
To family gathered from afar
Daughters carried
In your heart and arms,
Sons hugged
And kissed on cheeks
And shoulders

Nothing matches it–
The wealth of love
Displayed in gifts
And laughter,
The praise proclaimed
From elders' lips
In honor of the return

And there,
In the distant past
The present pours
Forth its gems, the fragrance
Of love come down
Bring gold and frankincense
Remember,
A Savior, too, was
Welcomed,
Nursed,
Loved,
Proclaimed.

(Valerie Bridgeman Davis, Epiphany, Years A, B, and C)

The Baptized Beloved

God was not ashamed to display deep affection for his Son. Shout it! Proclaim it! Declare it! Broadcast it! This is my Son, the Beloved, with whom I am well pleased. What an example–particularly for fathers today. The church has long been the place where people of color found nurture and affirmation. Look around you today. Is there some boy or girl who needs to hear a public pronouncement of godly adult love? Today is our opportunity to embrace the legacy of the church– by sharing God's love with people who most need it.

(Kwasi I. Kena, Baptism of the Lord, Year A)

Listen, Don't You Hear It?
(Isaiah 49:1-7)

Listen, don't you hear it?
The Lord is calling. Change the "when" of your hearing.
God doesn't need to wait until we're grown to speak.
God begins to call us before birth, while still in our mother's womb.

Listen, don't you hear it?
God not only calls us, God names us.
God forms our mouths to speak the pointed truth that nations and rulers and gang-bangers need to hear.

Listen, don't you hear it?
God speaks to us in dreams and visions and whispers destiny into our souls.
If we're vigilant, we'll hear what our purpose is in this world.

Listen, don't you hear it?
Too many of us are soul-deaf.

We miss those moments when God intersects our lives.
Too many youth are preoccupied with the death of their friends in the violent streets.

Listen, don't you hear it?
God is looking for willing servants to carry out a divine cause.
Divine causes can restore the broken hearted and the broken places.

Listen, don't you hear it?
God is calling you . . .

(Kwasi I. Kena, Second Sunday after Epiphany, Year A)

When Darkness Descends and Plods the Earth

(Isaiah 9:1-4)

When voluminous darkness descends and plods the earth
And your eyesight adjusts too comfortably to the dimness of sin
And your soul gropes wildly as if blind to righteousness

When putrefied darkness paints your face with moral decay
And people tell you "you've changed"
And you realize that you can't will yourself into "doing better"

When smothering darkness attempts to strangle the twinkle in the stars
And choke any hope in the future
And suffocate the last vestige of breath from your dreams

When it appears that the shadowy side of life has triumphed
Remember the words of the prophet Isaiah:

"The people who walked in darkness have seen a great light;
those who lived in a land of deep darkness—on them light has shined" (Isaiah 9:2).

(Kwasi I. Kena, Third Sunday after Epiphany, Year A)

Who Knows?

*(This poem may serve as a responsive reading, using the refrain of "Just a
Closer Walk with Thee" (no. 46 in* Songs of Zion*) between each stanza.
End with verse 3 of the hymn and the refrain.)*

What you see with your eyes is not what I am inside.
Words and tales passed from mouth to ear are often filled with lies.

You must never assume that I am *only* as I appear to be.
There are things beneath my surface, which you could never see.

Who knows what the future holds; do you know who I *really* am?

I could be a blessing in your life; maybe you're a blessing to me.
But never dismiss me for you don't know who I may be.

(Catrinia N. Harrison, Transfiguration Sunday, Year A)

Afterward

How do I cope when my heart is breaking?
How do I deal with the pain?
Not knowing the truth, confused by the deceit, I feel alone.
Around every corner a memory is made.
It grows harder to face each day.

The pieces of my world seem to have fallen apart;
I am trying to find the light.
An abyss of darkness has swallowed my heart;
I am struggling but losing the fight.

I long for joy and laughter.
Do I sit wanting, hoping, and waiting to have the "me" that was before?
Or do I wait and work for the "me" that will be formed after?
Abandonment by my Lord is hard to conceive.
I must overcome; I am going to succeed!

(Catrinia N. Harrison, First Sunday in Lent, Year A)

Make Us Like the Wind

Make us like the wind —ever-moving and ever moving others. And with joy we will dance with the leaves. In submission we will linger in the shade, cooling the skin of those scorched by the sun's heat. In awe we will pause and be still enough to hover over creation, admiring your world and waiting for your command. And when you move us, we will fly with more strength, reminding people that you are present even in times you may seem invisible. Breathe into our souls, Lord, and make us like the wind, like your Holy Spirit—in the name of Jesus Christ, Amen.

(Ciona D. Rouse, Second Sunday in Lent, Year A)

When Thirst Parches Your Soul

(Exodus 17:1-7)

When the thirst of life parches your soul, desperation sets in. It sets in hard, and you don't remember who God is or what God has done. That's just the truth. Desperation makes you believe you're going to die; it makes you test the limits of faith, and of ethics. It makes you blame the "Moses" in your life, the one who gave you the word of your deliverance from bondage. It makes the past struggles seem not so bad. Church becomes a wilderness. Relationships become wastelands. It all gets big. It's never just about you anymore when you're desperate. It's everything. It's everyone. It's the equivalent of "your children and your livestock." When your throat, your life, is parched, you want to stone the messengers. You argue and you test. You bargain and you beg. It's hard to trust who God is or what God has done. That's just the truth. And still, God provides: even when you're moaning and complaining; even when you're parched and pleading; even when your faith is a faint whisper from the past. God still provides. Disappointed in our desperation, maybe. Wishing we would remember the miraculous escapes we've had. But providing nonetheless. That's just the truth.

Look up; there's a rock gushing with refreshment for you somewhere in your life. Your past only sounds good because you can't see the future. There is a rock gushing somewhere in your life. That's just the truth. Look for it.

(Valerie Bridgeman Davis, Third Sunday in Lent, Year A)

I Came . . . But I had to Drag Myself Here

I came to worship today Lord, but I had to drag myself here. I find it hard to not be depressed. I have gone through another week without one affirmation of my uniqueness as an African American child of God. I have been bombarded by negative images of Black people. I have seen my people portrayed as criminals, drug dealers, and low achievers. But deep in my spirit, I know that there is another truth. Lord, I need you to speak to my spirit today and breathe new life into my soul. Come, Holy Spirit, Come!

(Junius Dotson, Fifth Sunday in Lent, Year A)

A Covenant in Plain Sight

(Isaiah 42:1-9)

In the still of night, we hold our breath, believing
One chosen, anointed will come, receiving
All our hopes; He will not break what in its weakness
Already is at the point of breaking, bruised and bleeding
A soft voice, blowing gently over ruins
He will lift a tender sound and settle in with truth
Never faltering or discouraged,
Establishing the one thing we need most
And do not know how to seek: justice–
Will flow from crowded cities and remote islands,
Creation will embrace the One who created
Heaven will touch where humans walk,
Angels tread where people spread their deepest dreams,
Dancing hand in hand with God
Searching for a light, a seed that roots in freedom
Opened eyes, captives freed, release
Only God will be the shine and we will see
What we have never seen before
A covenant divine, in plain sight.

(Valerie Bridgeman Davis, Holy Week, Year A)

Praise on the Streets

On this day, the whole city seemed to explode into praise on the streets while Jesus' enemies plotted his death in the shadows. As we celebrate Palm Sunday, we are reminded that not everyone rejoices to see truth ride unhindered through the streets. There will always be someone or something opposing the righteous. But we are also encouraged to look past the gloom and doom of Good Friday to the sure coming of the Resurrection. So, on this day of celebration, rejoice while you are able, 'cause trouble don't last always.

(Safiyah Fosua, Palm Sunday, Years A, B, C)

Who Stands after Falling?

"But Peter, standing with the eleven, raised his voice
and addressed them . . . "(Acts 2:14a)

Who stands up for the Lord after falling from grace? Who returns to ministry after being disgraced? Who tells others about salvation while being imperfect? Who would do such things?

Only a person who acknowledges the pain they've inflicted. Only a person who refuses to remain estranged from God. Only a person who believes that repentance is better than wallowing in self-pity. Only a person whom God has lifted from the gutter of life has the integrity to tell others about the love of the Lord.

Peter was such a person —are you?

(Kwasi I. Kena, Third Sunday of Easter, Year A)

One Tree Down to Its Very Roots

(Trinity Sunday)

There is a tree in Johannesburg, South Africa, that stands in the yard of a Catholic retreat center. When viewed from one angle, one sees a singular tree with a very large trunk. From another angle, the tree appears as three distinct trees, down to the very roots. The tree was nicknamed *Trinity–Three-in-One*. The base of the tree became a meeting ground where we experienced community. There, and around its trunks, we discussed the deep things of life. No matter where you leaned on the tree, you were supported. No matter where you gazed on it, it was beautiful–three trunks, one tree, inseparable and unified at its base, drawing us into fellowship with one another. It was amazing.

The existence of this tree is a natural and compelling illustration of the existence of our Triune God, a God that operates in community to create community. Whether calling out YHWH, Jesus, or Holy Spirit, it is the Three-in-One God, inseparable and unified, that responds to our every need. No matter what name or office you call out, God will bear you up. No matter where you look, you can see the beauty of what God is doing.

God the Creator; God the Savior; God Who Empowers: lures us into loving relationship with God's self and with one another. It is just so amazing! Look again; it is one tree down to its very roots.

(Marilyn E. Thornton, Trinity Sunday, Year A)

Sometimes We're Tested

(Genesis 22:1-14)

From time to time, God tests us–as Abraham was tested–to see just how much we trust God and how much we can be trusted with God's future plans and blessings for humankind. God tests us to see if, like Martin King and Mandela, Sojourner and Bethune, we will make ourselves available to God's deeper calling on our lives. You may very well be tested to see just how faithful you are to God and God's mission for your life and the lives of others.

Our lives are punctuated by sacrifices–sacrifices of our time, sacrifices of our energies, sacrifices that affect our families, sacrifices now, with the hope of a better future. God shows us where God wants us to be, what God wants us to do. As we, like Abraham, look up and see God's possibilities, even in the depths of our trials and tribulations, our sufferings and shames, we will be able to respond with hope, like Abraham, knowing that the worship of God will sustain us in the test.

And so, we continue in readiness to sacrifice. Sometimes we work two and three jobs so that our young'uns can get an education. Sometimes we burn the midnight oil so that our dreams and the dreams of others will come to pass. Sometimes we position ourselves to give up the very thing we love, so that God can do far more with that love than we ever dreamed of. But we go, as children of God we go, like ancestors of the Motherland, who remember that we've come this far by faith, leaning on the Lord, trusting in God's Holy Word. God has never failed us yet, so we go.

We go: trusting and believing that the Lord will make a way somehow. The Lord will provide. And as we go, and as we do what the Lord says do, God intervenes in the midst of our tests. God shows up in the midst of our trials. Well done, my good and faithful servant. Now I know you fear God. And there are rewards for passing tests, you know. When we do not withhold anything or anybody from God, God will take what we have offered, bless it, prosper it, expand it, and increase it for the betterment of generations and generations to come. From time to time, like Abraham and multitudes in our African ancestry, God tests us. But tests become testimonies for those who remain faithful. Have faith in God today and we will receive the reward of a diligent seeker.

(Joseph W. Daniels, Jr., Sixth Sunday after Pentecost, Year A)

Fighting the Frenzy

(Matthew 11:28-30)

When did the frenzy begin?
When did it become more virtuous
   to rip and tear and run than to be silent before God?
When did we decide that it was better to wear out than to rust out?
Who told us to keep church people so busy lest they stop coming to church?
Somebody tell me when did the frenzy begin?

Perhaps we caught it from the culture
a frenzied culture
stuck in motion
frozen in busyness
intent on movement.

No matter where we got it
we can't seem to stop.
Wear your watch
beat the clock
be on time
never time to rest.

look at the words of Jesus
Come to me all you that are weary

yes we are weary,
we have worn ourselves out,
like boxers beating the air
always struggling, always flailing,
hardly ever connecting with our goals.

Come to me, all you that are weary.

(Safiyah Fosua, Seventh Sunday after Pentecost, Year A)

Generous Quietude

(Matthew 11:28-30)

Carry a little quiet inside you
while the world continues
in rush and rage
fighting and frenzy.

Carry a little quiet inside you
so that the worry and war
trouble and tumult
do not capture you in their grip

Tarry in the Son-filled meadow of the heart
beside the still waters
where God's Spirit refreshes and renews

Carry so much quiet inside you
that you have some extra calm
to share with me.

(Safiyah Fosua, Seventh Sunday after Pentecost, Year A)

Prayer of Intercession for a Spouse

(Genesis 24:34-38, 42-49, 58-67)

(May be used as an intercessory prayer or as a meditation printed in the bulletin.)

Our Lord and our God, we approach you this morning in your sovereignty and your grace, thanking you for being our guide, our wisdom, our strength, our all and all. We come before you in the name of Jesus to intercede on behalf of those who seek to find Spirit-filled, Spirit-guided, and Spirit-directed companionship today. God, you know more than all of us the tensions that exist between Black men and Black women when it comes to relationships. God, you know very clearly the hurt and pain, the anguish and the shame, the torment and the game. These things have given birth to devastating relationships.

Lord, we come before you, confessing that we have participated in drama and chaos. We've played games with others, and we've been burned by others. Some of us have even been left at the altar in tears and in turmoil because we did not take time to find your will for our lives.

Today, we turn away from sharing men and keeping harems. We turn away from casual intimacy and ungodly friendships. God, position us this day for blessing. Help us to be men and women who listen for your voice. Teach us to love ourselves and to respect each other. Let our relationships be a testimony of your goodness, your grace, and your power to order our lives, order our relationships, and bring peace to our homes. This, God, is our prayer. This, God, is our hope. This, God, is our joyful expectation in your name. Amen.

(Joseph W. Daniels, Jr., Seventh Sunday after Pentecost, Year A)

Still God Sows
(Matthew 13:1-23)

What can be compared to God's faithfulness? In spite of "thorny" receptions, God continues to sow good news. Forgiveness, grace, love, and comfort all come from God's hand with the hope that someone will receive them.

God sows tirelessly, knowing that distractions prevent many seeds from sprouting. Doubt barges into our thoughts. Impatience taunts our faith saying, "Why not give up because God has not answered yet?"

Still God sows, hoping that we will be the "good soil" that chooses to believe, endure, and bear good fruit.

(Kwasi I. Kena, Eighth Sunday after Pentecost, Year A)

Lord, Is that You?
(Genesis 28:10-19a)

Lord was that you,
when life shoved me, and I stumbled but did not fall?
Lord was that you,
when my child went astray, and I worried but still managed to hope?
Lord is that you,
encouraging me to overcome self-doubt and go back to school?
Lord is that you,
keeping my family together while my spouse serves active duty overseas?

Surely the Lord is with me throughout each day–even when I do not know it.

(Kwasi I. Kena, Ninth Sunday after Pentecost)

Who Weeds the Garden?
Musings about the Parable of the Weeds and the Wheat
(Matthew 13:2-30, 36-43)

(May be used as a dramatic reading before or after the gospel is read.)

Who wants to weed the garden?

"I will," volunteered the lady in the large hat with a screeching voice that sounded like a fingernail on a chalkboard.

"I will," volunteered the quiet young man.

"I will," volunteered the preacher whose harsh words had run many a seeker out the front door.

"I will," volunteered the Crusader, who was always looking for a new cause to beat with his Bible.

The gardener looked up at the crowd that had gathered around him while he stooped to cover the roots of a seedling with moist soil. "Why ya'll want to weed this garden?" he asked without standing. He hadn't asked the question, but he had certainly heard them talking about it as they approached him.

"Gertie," he said to the woman with the large hat, "I remember when you last tried to weed the garden. You couldn't tell an onion from a dandelion!"

Laughter.

"And, John," he said to the quiet young man, "your eyes are always closed; you keep them closed so much that *regular light* seems to blind you. I'd be afraid to let you weed my garden."

Laughter.

"And you preacher," he said with a laugh, "unless you mistook 'pluck grapes' for 'preach gospel,' maybe you should leave the gardening to me."

More laughter!

Finally, the gardener stood and cautiously looked the Crusader in the eye. "If you had it your way," he said, "there would be no plant in this garden that you did not plant; and you would pull all the plants that were not the same height!"

Silence.

"Who weeds this garden?" After a long pause, the gardener said: *"Onliest person gets to weed this garden is God!"*

With that, he turned from them and walked toward his barn to feed the animals

(Safiyah Fosua, Ninth Sunday after Pentecost, Year A)

Who Tricks the Trickster?
(Genesis 29:15-28)

Tricked! I have labored long and hard only to be denied what is due me. Tricked! The "powers that be" took advantage of me, and I could only agree to more labor—because I loved what the powers possessed. I can endure much for love's sake. I can live on promised hope for years.

Still I am not forever duped. For my name, Jacob, means trickster. I can be fooled only once. Perhaps I refrain from retaliation because I appreciate the guile of Laban. Given the same opportunity, I may have done the same. Ask my brother Esau.

Lord, only you can free me from the vicious cycle that transforms me from prey to predator.

(Kwasi I. Kena, Tenth Sunday after Pentecost, Year A)

You Give Them Something to Eat
(Matthew 14:13-21)

When Jesus went ashore, "he saw a great crowd and had compassion for them and cured their sick." When the disciples came to Jesus and urged him to dismiss the crowds, Jesus said to them, "They need not go away; you give them something to eat."

So many hunger today . . .
(Multiple voices)
They passed over me for promotion—again.
They consume what I offer without as much as a thank you.
They don't call or write or visit me.
They tire of caring for me because I can't get well.

Jesus left the people of the world in the hands of his disciples. The people need not go away; you give them something to eat.

(Kwasi I. Kena, Eleventh Sunday after Pentecost, Year A)

It Takes Fire

(Exodus 3:1-15)

It took a miraculous fire to get my attention. No loss of life. No burned out homes. No crowds to gawk and gaze. It was a private fire meant only for me.

"Come."
"Here I am."

"Not too close. Remove your shoes. This place is holy."

God puts holy fire into our mouths to speak truth to power. How long will bullies frighten children? How long will "higher-ups" oppress the rank and file? How long will drug dealers hook innocents? How long will companies lose workers' pensions? How long will people die in senseless conflict?

As long as fire in holy places goes unnoticed . . . and cool smoke rises where Christian passion once burned.

Sing: This is Holy Ground.

(Kwasi I. Kena, Thirteenth Sunday after Pentecost, Year A)

A Good Reason to Shine

(1 Thessalonians 5:1-11)

Children of light you have reason to shine!
Christ is your light.
and, while he tarries,
you are the light of the world!
Children of light, you were *made* to shine
made and remade in the image of God
made to reflect the light of the Burning Sun
made to receive light, and to give it off.
Children of light, you'd *better* shine
for the Son of Righteousness comes
looking for light; looking for *your* light
on that great Day of the Lord.

(Safiyah Fosua Twenty-sixth Sunday after Pentecost, Year A)

Rhythm Band

(Psalm 150:1-6)

I've got a tambourine in my bosom. It's beating out praises to God my King. No one else can hear it, but it beats out a rhythm that says, "Praise You. Thank You, Lord!" Its bells shake and accentuate time when I walk through the produce section at the grocery store. Its skin is well worn from praising the Lord.

I've got a trumpet in my heart. It sings with sweet brassy notes. It soars through holy melodies while I'm riding in my car. Flourishes and salutes, blue notes and high notes reach toward the heavens to worship my Lord.

I've got a harp in my hands. Its gentle notes are strummed as I sit at my desk. My hands caress each string each time I think of Him. No one else hears the music as I reach for the harp strings; but its melodious sounds and chords reverberate through my soul. Holy Spirit take control.

The brass drum is in my belly. With each beat of the bass, I bend and sway and reach out in adoration. That drum beats when I walk down the street. It gives me purpose and coaxes my feet to gently pound the pavement. My neck begins to bob in response to its otherwise inaudible beat. I beat the drum down the street.

There is dancing in my feet as I wait for the bus. Left-side-sway-step! Heh! Right-side-sway-step! Just like the choir—along with the choir. There's a rhythm band on the inside of me; there's music in the air; there's dancing in my feet! Praise you, my King. Let everything that has breath praise the Lord.

(Excerpt from Mother Wit *by Safiyah Fosua (c)1996 by Abingdon Press. Used by permission.)*

Shoulder to Shoulder

(Psalm 133:1-3)

I sat between
    Two noble ladies today
While we were shoulder to shoulder in church.
The day was hot
    Sweat-rings formed around my neck
While
Two noble ladies shouldered me
    On the Lord's day.

On my left shoulder
    Sat a women
    About forty-five years old.
The laughter lines etched around her eyes
    Were there from years of practice.
Her eyes laughed a greeting my way
    While we sat there
Shoulder to shoulder.
All through the service, she had
    Happy feet
    Happy hands
    Happy hair
    Happy smiles!

Happy rubs off when you sit so close.
    Before long, I was happy too!
    I was happy to be there
    Shouldered with this woman.
    Happy for her laughing eyes
    Glad for the songs, which made my feet get happy
    Happy for the words of life
        Flowing out to me.

On the other side
    Sat an old saint
    Barely able to move in response

To the moving of the Holy Ghost
Which stirred our very souls.
She shouldered me gently
   I gentled her shoulder
   Which was bowed and stooped with age.
   I gentled her leathery hands
   Which barely gripped mine in greeting
And reached for her gentle smile
   When she offered it to me.

Her eyes were squinted with age
   And wrinkle-worn from seeing
   Things I had yet to see.

Everything
   About this woman
   Cried experience and wisdom.

I longed to have the wisdom
   That was on my right side

Infect me as did the happiness on my left side.

As we all sat shoulder to shoulder on the Lord's day.

(Excerpt from Mother Wit *by Safiyah Fosua
(c)1996 by Abingdon Press. Used by permission.)*

We Are One

(Ephesians 2:17)

There is some strange thread that binds us together.
It enables us to set our feet
   In the house of the Lord
   In Mississippi
   Or Los Angeles
     And feel at home.

This thread is stronger
Than the Baptist Church
Or the Church of God in Christ;
Stronger than an order of worship
Or a theological dispute
Regardless of the different creeds we may confess,
   Or the names on the front of our churches
     We are one!

Shouting together,
   We try to make heaven our home.
From the Zion churches of South Africa
   To the New Testament churches of the West Indies,
     We sing familiar songs.
Choirs sway and rock
   To familiar rhythms in West Africa.

The Mothers of the Church
   Are sitting together
   And wearing white
     In Bahia,
       Chicago
         And Egypt.
They shout their amens in unison.

Children scoot around on splintery floorboards
   In Washington, D.C.
     And New Orleans; while chalky cement floors
       Make ashy knees in Haiti.

The women's choir comes together,

Dressed like dozens of twin sisters
And singing likes angels on Women's Sunday.
All the while,
   Pots bubble,
     Fowls fry,
        And old ladies set the table for dinner.

We dance the Peacock Strut,
   The Stretch,
     and the Old-Mother's-Three-Step
       Together, to an invisible beat.

Who taught so many of us
   To form protective circles
     Around one another
       When the Spirit begins to move?

What unseen strings
   Pull that right palm to the sky,
     As Jesus passes by?

We learned these things
From God our Father, while
In Mother Africa's womb,
For we are one.

(From Mother Wit *by Abena Safiyah Fosua.*
Copyright © 1996 by Abingdon Press, Nashville, TN.)

Calls to Worship, Invocations, and Gathering Words

Surely We Are in the House of the Lord!

My soul smiles
My heart dances
My fears flee
My mind wrestles
My tongue shouts praise
My loneliness finds company
My spirit meets God
Surely, we are in the house of the Lord!

(Ciona D. Rouse) First Sunday in Advent, 2004, Year A)

Oh, How Good Is Unity!
(Psalm 133)

One: Oh how good and pleasant it is when we live together in unity!

Many: We come together Lord.

One: We come as people who are rich and poor, young and old.

Many: We come together Lord.

One: We come as people freed from addiction and actively seeking recovery.

Many: We come together Lord.

One: We come as people who are united by your great love for us.

Many: We lay aside our differences before a merciful God. We come together in unity Lord.

All: Hallelujah! Hallelujah!

(Junius Dotson, Second Sunday in Advent, 2004, Year A)

Jesus Is Coming!

All: He's coming, Jesus is coming!

I will kick the dirt off my shoes
Then I will sweep the dust from my porch
It's time to get my life fresh and clean.

All: He's coming, Jesus is coming!

(Ciona D. Rouse, Second Sunday in Advent, 2004, Year A)

Gathering

One:
Joy indescribable,
Hope unbelievable,
Love inconceivable came down to earth!

All:
We gather excitedly,
We stand expectantly;
We wait patiently for Christ to come again!

(Ciona D. Rouse, Third Sunday in Advent, 2004, Year A)

Grace, Grace! God's Grace!

(This call is not to be printed; only the leader has a copy.
Tell the congregation, "Please respond any way you wish, if you have expe-
rienced this.")

Grace! Grace! God's grace! Is God's grace sufficient for you?
(Congregational response)

Grace! Grace! God's Grace!
Does God's grace give you the strength you need?
(Congregational response)

Did God's grace wake you up this morning?
(Congregational response)

Did God's grace start you on your way?
(Congregational response)

Does God's grace make you love all of your enemies?
(Congregational response)

Do you believe God's grace will give you the victory?
(Congregational response)

Then let's worship the God of Grace and God of Glory!

(Sherrie Dobbs Johnson, Third Sunday after Advent, Year)

Let Us Adore Christ

One: O come let us adore him.

Many: Like the Magi of old, we lift our voices and praise the savior of the world.

One: O come let us adore him.

Many: Like ancient Israel, we proclaim the kindness of the Lord, his deeds and all that the Lord has done for us.

One: O come let us adore him.

Many: Like believers of old, we rejoice that Jesus loves us, has mercy on us, and redeems us.

All: O Come let us adore him, Christ the Lord.

(Kwasi I. Kena, The Sunday after Christmas, Year A)

Arise! Shine!

(Isaiah 61)

One: Arise! Shine!

Many: God's light has come to reveal The Way in this New Year.

One: Arise! Shine!

Many: The glory of the Lord has risen upon us.

One: Arise! Shine!

Many: God's light penetrates the darkness that covers the world.

One: Arise! Shine!

Many: Nations shall come to God's light and kings to the brightness of God's dawn.

All: Arise! Shine! For the Glory of the Lord has risen upon us.

(Kwasi I. Kena, First Sunday, Epiphany, Year A)

Light of God, Illumine

Invocation

Light of God, illumine the path that leads us to healing, hope, and salvation. Glory of God, fill this sanctuary and expose the darkness that stalks our souls. Light of God, shine with such brightness that we marvel in awe.

Glory of God, fill each temple of the Holy Spirit present today.

Light of God, Glory of God, we welcome you in this place.

(Kwasi I. Kena, Epiphany Sunday, Year A)

Let Us Raise Our Voices

Opening Sentences

(1 Corinthians 1:2)

To the church in *[insert the name of your city]*
Located on *[insert church's street name]* **street**
To make a difference
To those sanctified in Christ Jesus
Saved to serve humbly and dependably
To those called to be holy
Serving as living witnesses of God's transforming grace

Let us raise our voices unashamedly
Rivaling heaven's angels
To praise our Lord and Savior Jesus Christ
Let us lift every voice and sing to our Master and Maker.

(Kwasi I. Kena, Second Sunday after Epiphany, Year A)

Standing in Your House

She pulled the covers over her head, Lord, and cried out to you the other night.
And she stands in your house today.

He yelled at his lover, Lord, and called her anything but *beloved*.
And he stands in your house today.

Lord, two days ago, she was tempted to steal, to be violent, to lie.
And she stands in your house today.

He thought of suicide last night, Lord, didn't want to see another sunrise.
And he stands in your house today.

Lord, Lord, she housed terrible thoughts about her neighbor, and spread rumors she knew were untrue.
And she stands in your house today.

Lord, he decided to start a new relationship, with a woman he knew was not his wife.
And he stands in your house today.

Last week, Lord, she made it through initiation and is now in a gang family.
And she stands in your house today.

A month ago, Lord, he refused to take *no* from the girl next door.
And he stands in your house today.

Two years ago, Lord, she was single and pregnant and decided not to give birth.
And she stands in your house today.

We stand in your house messy, confused, and desperate for you.
We choose to worship you, and in our glory and our shame, you say to us,
"Come. There is room for everyone."
So we stand in your house today!

(Ciona D. Rouse, General Call, Year A)

I've Got a Feeling . . .

(Psalm 46:1-11)

(The Spiritual may be sung as a part of the litany.)

One: I've got a feeling, everything's gonna be alright!

Many: Somebody's hurting, somebody's in pain.
    Been a hard week of struggle and strain.
    Many a worry, many a care,
    If God is God, is God aware?

One: I've got a feeling, everything's gonna be alright!

Many: War overseas, shooting in our streets
    Kids dying every day, old folk left alone weak.
    Too much happening
    To handle on our own.
    Family problems, job concerns,
    Body's failing, can't you hear the moans?

One: I've got a feeling, everything's gonna be alright!

Many: Got here troubled, entered with trials.
    Tired of walking so many lonely miles.
    Empty promises from leaders all around.
    Can we usher in a different sound?

One: Jesus done told me, everything's gonna be alright!

Many: Is there hope in this hopeless domain,
    For Blacks, Latinos, Asians, Europeans just the same?
    Hurt knows no color, ethnicity no shame.
    There's got to be a better way. No one likes living lame.

One: Jesus done told me, everything's gonna be alright!

Many: There is a way that our elders came
    Whenever, they traveled that way, they were never the same.
    Momma told us about it, Daddy too.
    The generations said there's help, when we just worship the name.

One: Jesus done told me, everything's gonna be alright!

Many: I'm so glad that trouble don't last always,
I'm reminded in the good book where it says,
God is our refuge and our strength, a very present help
in times like these.
Lord, we need you to visit us, would you graciously do so please.

One: Oh, oh, oh, holy ghost done told me, everything's gonna be alright.

Many: In the time of trouble,
The Savior is here.
Oh, come let us adore him,
In him, lay your fears.

All: be alright, be alright, be alright.

(Joseph W. Daniels, Jr., General, Year A)

Come, Holy Spirit, We Are Ready . . .

One: Let us enter in the courts of your sanctuary. Let us release to you the fears and dangers that entrap our identity

Many: Come, Holy Spirit.

One: We release to you the tears that streak our faces from the disappointments and pains of a broken society.

Many: Come, Holy Spirit.

One: We open our hearts to release the resounding impact of hatred and envy.

Many: Come, Holy Spirit.

One: We are ready to receive your word and respectfully respond to the glory of your goodness.

Many: Come, Holy Spirit.

One: We will embrace your joy!

Many: Come Holy Spirit.

All: Thank you Holy Spirit, we are in awe of your presence.

(Carolyn W. Dandridge, General, Year A)

We Praise You, Not Because . . .

Opening Sentences

We praise you!
Not because we are worthy
But because you are worthy

We praise you!
Not just with our voices today
But with our living everyday

We praise you!
Not because it pleases us
But because it pleases you

We praise you!

(Ciona D. Rouse, Third Sunday in Lent, Year A)

The Lord Is My Shepherd

(Psalm 23)

One: The world offers busy schedules and more stuff to do, but God offers rest.
Many: The Lord is my Shepherd; I shall not be in want!

One: The world offers faster cars and bigger houses, but God offers comfort.
Many: The Lord is my Shepherd; I shall not be in want!

One: The world offers war and terror, but God offers protection.
Many: The Lord is my Shepherd; I shall not be in want!

One: The world offers cheap love and cheap thrills, but God offers goodness and mercy.
Many: The Lord is My Shepherd; I shall not be in want!

All: Come now and let us dwell in the house of the Lord!

(Junius Dotson, Fourth Sunday in Lent, Year A)

Lord, Raise Us Up!

One: We come, knowing that we are living in the midst of dead relationships.
Many: Lord, Raise Us Up!

One: We come troubled by dead finances.
Many: Lord, Raise Us Up!

One: We come with hopes and dreams that have died.
Many: Lord, Raise Us Up!

One: We come, Lord, to be revived in your presence.
All: Lord, Raise us up, and breathe new life into our spirits!

(Junius Dotson, Fifth Sunday in Lent, Year A)

Gathering Words

We sing Hosanna! Throughout the world, we the people of God, gather with branches in our hands. We gather singing Hosanna! Blessed is the One who comes in the name of the Lord! Hosanna in the highest! Blessed be God forever and forever! Let us worship God.

(Valerie Bridgeman Davis, Palm Sunday, Year A)

Call to Worship

One: O Magnify the Lord with me, and let us exalt God's name together!

Many: We enter in, singing and dancing, with palm branches in our hands!

(Valerie Bridgeman Davis, Palm Sunday, Year A)

Invocation

No one but you, our God, can mend our hearts and strengthen our resolve. No one but you can help us see your salvation. Come, Holy One! Come, Hope of Zion! Come! Receive our worship! Come! Hear our prayers! Come! Answer and save! Come! We are waiting! Come! Hear our hearts' cries! Come! We are ready! Come! We are waiting! Come!

(Valerie Bridgeman Davis, Palm Sunday, Year A)

Call to Worship
(Psalm 118)

One: O, Give thanks to the Lord who is GOOD!!!

Many: God's steadfast love lasts forever

One: O, Give thanks to God at all times

Many: God's mercy is everlasting

All: O, Give thanks; for God is good, God is good!

(Valerie Bridgeman Davis, Palm Sunday, Year A)

Ride On!

*(Followed by singing the Traditional Version of
"Ride On, King Jesus" #77 Songs of Zion)*

Rejoice greatly, O daughter Zion! Shout aloud, O daughter Jerusalem! Look, your king comes to you. (Zechariah 9:9a NRSV)
Ride on, King Jesus, no one can hinder you!

Look, your king comes to you; triumphant and victorious is he, humble and riding on a donkey, on a colt, the foal of a donkey. (Zechariah 9:9b NRSV)
Ride on, King Jesus, no one can hinder you!

See the crowd coming into the city! Join the glad procession with songs of praise.
Ride on, King Jesus, no one can hinder you!

We come, lifting our palm branches shouting, "Hosanna to the Son of David! Blessed is the one who comes in the name of the Lord! Hosanna in the highest heaven!" (Matthew 21:9b NRSV)
Ride on, King Jesus, no one can hinder you!

On this holy day, we come with lifted hands, waving palms, and raised voices to proclaim that you are the King of Kings and the Lords of Lords!
Ride on, King Jesus, no one can hinder you!

(Safiyah Fosua, Palm Sunday, Year A)

Let Us Praise the Lord, Who . . .

(Psalm 16)

One: Come! Let us praise the Lord who counsels
Many: Let us praise the Lord, who speaks in the night
One: Let us praise the Lord, who calls in the day
Many: Let us praise the Lord and not be shaken
All: Let us praise the Lord forever more!

(Valerie Bridgeman Davis, Second Sunday of Easter, Year A)

Call on the Lord Who Bends Low to Hear Us

(Psalm 116)

One: Come! Lift your voices to the Lord who always hears us.

Many: Listen Lord. Hear our voices sing your praises.

One: Call on the Lord who bends low to hear us.

Many: Listen Lord. We lift our voices to you in praise.

One: Call on the name of the Lord, all people.

Many: Listen Lord. We call on your wonderful name.
For you saved us, you raised us and turned our lives around.
Let your name be praised in this congregation.

(Kwasi I. Kena, Third Sunday of Easter, Year A)

We Are the Church

Gathering Call

*(Cheer led by the youth with pom-poms,
followed by "We Are the Church," 558, The United Methodist Hymnal)*

Youth:

**We are the church,
The mighty, mighty church!
Everywhere we go-o,
People want to know-o,
Who we a-re,
What we do-oo,
So we tell them:
We are the ch-urch,
The mighty, mighty, ch-urch!**

Leader: We are the church, the mighty, mighty church!
We were built on Christ the Solid Rock.
The Good Shepherd called us into this place, name by name.

Youth:

**We are the church,
The mighty, mighty church!
Everywhere we go-o,
People want to know-o,
Who we a-re,
What we do-oo,
So we tell them:
We are the ch-urch,
The mighty, mighty, ch-urch!**

Leader: We recognize the voice of The Good Shepherd
who walks with us and talks with us.
We recognize the voice of The Good Shepherd
who is the guardian of our souls.
We recognize the voice of The Good Shepherd
who leads us in the path of righteousness.
We recognize the voice of The Good Shepherd

who picks us up from the squalor, brushes us off,
bids us to straighten up and fly right!
We recognize the voice of The Good Shepherd
who has made it possible for us to have it all,
even if we have nothing.
His peace gives us abundant life. And so we say with joy:

Youth, congregation, and leader:

We are the church,
The mighty, mighty church of Christ!
Everywhere we want people to know just how much He loves you and
me!

(Sherrie Dobbs Johnson, Fourth Sunday of Easter, Year A)

Always Room for One More

(Based on the Spiritual "Plenty Good Room")

One: There's always room in God's house for one more.

**Many:
There's plenty good room!
Plenty good room!
Plenty good room in God's House!***

One: This place where we gather is filled with good things: companionship and familiarity; warmth and security; support and encouragement. We've come to claim our seat in God's House.

**Many:
There's plenty good room!
Plenty good room!
Plenty good room in God's House!***

One: We have entered into these doors. Our host, Jesus Christ, has called us to the house name by name. Evil is not welcomed here. Our host is on patrol for it. Our host, Christ Jesus, works day and night to rescue us from the Evil that awaits us. Our host, Christ Jesus deputizes us to arrest Evil wherever we find it. He trains us for gracious combat. In God's house, built by Jesus Christ, we are trained to fight hate with love, and greed with generosity. Let those who are sad come and claim their joy! Let those who are scared come and claim their boldness! Let those who are frustrated come and claim their confidence.

**Many:
There's plenty good room!
Plenty good room!
Plenty good room in God's House!**

*(Author's original version of last sentence that connects with the opening hymn, *Plenty Good Room in my Father's Kingdom*.)

(Sherrie Dobbs Johnson, Fourth Sunday of Easter, Year A)

Nothing Is As Great As You

Invocation

Oh God, you are a mighty God! Nothing is as great as you. You overturn evil. You hand out justice and blessings. For you, the impossible is possible. You can even make those who died live again!

When you brought back Jesus from the dead, you did so to show us just how powerful you are and how much you love us. You sent the Good Shepherd to show us the way to please you. You sent the Good Shepherd to show us how to love one another. You returned him from the dead to show us that you forgive our cowardliness and cruelty. We know you expect more from us.

Continue to guide us, O Mighty God. Do not take your hand from us. Send into our lives people who are like angels to keep watch over us, to keep us from harming others or being harmed. Make us your angels. Make us one people with the entire world, united by the blood and love of the Good Shepherd, Jesus Christ. Amen.

(Sherrie Dobbs Johnson, Fourth Sunday of Easter, Year A)

Come, Lord Jesus, Speak . . .

One: Come, Lord Jesus, speak to us in parables and rhyme.
Many: For you are an intergenerational Savior.

One: Come, Lord Jesus, let us again hear some *old-time religion.*
Many: For you are the Savior of all the ages.

One: Come, Lord Jesus, speak quietly to us.
Many: For your Spirit speaks through the wind.

One: Come, Lord Jesus, speak loudly to us.
Many: For your Spirit speaks through the thunder.

All: Savior of all age groups, languages, and cultures, we await your voice.

(Sherrie Boyens-Dobbs, Sixth Sunday of Easter, Year A)

Centering Prayer

Lord, we've come this morning seeking your presence, but it's hard to settle in when so many things cloud our minds. Even in Your House, it's hard to pay attention. We are here trusting that you will get our attention, through some song sung, some witness raised, some scripture unfolded, some gesture offered.

All: Come, Lord Jesus, lift us up by your Holy Spirit. Amen.

(Sherrie Boyens-Dobbs, Seventh Sunday of Easter or Ascension Sunday, Year A)

Open Your Hand to Us, O God

O Lord, how manifold are your works! In wisdom you have made them all. Open your hand to us, O God, giver of good things. Do not hide your face from us. Should you remove your Spirit from us, we shall surely return to the dust. Send forth your Spirit in this worship service today and let us be re-created. Renew us, O God, with your spirit.

(To use as an invocation, end here with)
In Jesus' name. Amen.

(Marilyn E. Thornton, the Day of Pentecost, Year A)

From our Cries for Deliverance
(Unison Prayer)

**From our cries for deliverance in the wilderness of Egypt,
to our pleas for mercy in the Middle Passage,
from our moans for your grace to appear in the Movement,
to our present pleas for hope in desperate times,
God, nothing has been too hard for you.**

**Our Lord and our God,
as we assemble in this sanctuary,
grateful for another day of life,
thankful for another chance to worship your holy name,
we call on you,
pleading with you to come and sit with us as we assemble in your sanctuary.**

(Joseph W. Daniels, Jr., Fourth Sunday after Pentecost, Year A)

Lord, We Call on You

Invocation

(Psalm 86:1-10)

Our Lord and our God, we call on you this day asking you to be present with us and to visit us in this our time of trouble.

Lord, we are poor and needy materially.
For many of us, there is more month at the end of the money,
than money at the end of the month.
Many of us are living from paycheck to paycheck.
Lord, we call upon you right now to help us and guide us.

Lord, we are poor and needy spiritually.
We have cheated you of the time you desire from us.
We have turned away from having a healthy, intimate relationship with you.
Our prayer lives, meditation lives, study lives, giving lives, have given way to
the demands made of us by the world, the job, and creature comforts of life.
Lord, we ask you to be with us this day.

Lord, we call upon the power of your Holy Spirit,
• To comfort us in our time of trial
• To guard us in our great hour of weakness
• To have mercy on us in our many moments of anguish.

Lord, would you bring us joy today?
Would you lift our souls from sorrow?
There is none like you, O Lord.
And so we beseech you to hear our prayer.

We invite you to come and be present with us.
We look to you for answers.
We trust you in the time of trouble.
We acknowledge your greatness.

We await your mercies and give you thanks even before they come.
Amen.

(Joseph W. Daniels, Jr., Fifth Sunday after Pentecost, Year A)

Opening Sentences

(Romans 6:1b-11)

Just as you are no longer a slave in society, you are no longer a slave to sin. Just as your ancestors were emancipated years ago, you've been freed to live with Christ. You are dead to sin, and alive in Christ. So *be* free indeed.

(Joseph W. Daniels, Jr., Fifth Sunday after Pentecost, Year A)

We Welcome Those Who Have Come

(Matthew 10:40-42)

Lord, just as you have welcomed us when we were strangers with no home, just as you have taken us in when others said, "No," we ourselves seek to welcome those who have come to worship and praise your holy name. We welcome you this morning in this place to sit down and be present with us. Let us worship God!

(Joseph W. Daniels, Jr., Sixth Sunday after Pentecost, Year A)

Come on Ya'll, Let's Worship the Lord!
(Matthew 11:16-19, 25-30)

One: Come on ya'll, let's worship the Lord!
Come to Jesus, all you who have suffered a *beat down* this week.

Many: Come to Jesus, all you who have experienced family turmoil this week.

One: Come to Jesus, all you who are tired of the Iraqi War, tired of $2.25 (insert most recent price) gas, tired of glass ceilings, quotas, minimum wage jobs, and limited family values.

Many: Come to Jesus, all you who have a job that is getting on your last nerve.

One: Jesus said, "I'll give you rest. I'll bring you relief. I'll provide your deliverance. I'll make a way."

Many: And Jesus will give us wonderful rest!

All: Come on ya'll, let's worship the Lord!

(Joseph W. Daniels, Jr., Seventh Sunday after Pentecost, Year A)

Lamp to My Feet, Light to My Path
(Psalm 119:105-112)

One: Your word is a lamp to my feet.

Many: Show my feet where the righteous walk.
Protect me from evil and prod me to fight for justice.
Guide me past temptation and compel me to help someone in need.

One: Your word is a light to my path.

Many: Light my path when I have to walk alone through dark alleys,
empty parking lots, and deserted streets.

One: When we are afflicted, give us life Lord.

Many: Give us life when misery dulls our souls.
Give us life when sorrow swallows hope.
Give us life when persecution pummels sanity.

One: Accept our offering of praise, Lord.

Many: Praise you Lord–Lamp to my feet, Light to my path, Giver of life.

(Kwasi I. Kena, Eighth Sunday after Pentecost, Year A)

Praise God for Hope-filled Dreams

One: Despite hardship, our ancestors dared to dream God-sized dreams.
Many: Praise God for hope-filled dreams.

One: Do it again, Lord. Dream big dreams through us today!
Many: Praise God for new dreams for our generation.

One: Invisible God, be visible through our faith today.
Many: Praise God who empowers us with faith to see what others miss.

One: Will we stop building a better future because of evil?
Many: No! Our God will deliver us from evil!

One: Will we concede our neighborhoods because evil walks the streets?
Many: No God will judge all evildoers!

All: Come now, Lord, and fulfill your dreams in us today!

(Kwasi I. Kena, Ninth Sunday after Pentecost, Year A)

Let Praise Spring from Your Lips

(Psalm 105:1-11, 45b)

Men: O give thanks to the Lord. Call on God's name.
Women: Tell the world the great things God has done.

Men: Sing to the Lord, sing praises to God.
Women: Let your soul look up in wonder and sing, "How I Got Over."

Men: Glory in God's holy name.
Women: Let every heart that seeks the Lord declare God's glory.

Men: Seek God and God's strength.
Women: Seek the Lord continually. Let praise spring from your lips.

All: Praise God from whom all blessings flow.

(Kwasi I. Kena, Tenth Sunday after Pentecost, Year A)

Nothing Shall Separate Us Today

(Romans 8:35-38)

One: Let nothing stand between you and God today!
Many: We have come to lift you up O God,
Let nothing separate us from you!

One: Not danger in the streets
Or concern over what to eat!
Many: We have come to lift you up O God,
Let nothing separate us from you!

One: Not a fight with your friend
Or work that will not end
Many: We have come to lift you up O God,
Let nothing separate us from you!

One: Lord we come before you today convinced
Many: that neither death, nor life, nor angels, nor rulers, nor things present, nor things to come, nor powers, nor height, nor depth, nor anything else in all creation, will be able to separate us from the love of God in Christ Jesus our Lord! (Romans 8:38-39 NRSV)

(Safiyah Fosua, Tenth Sunday after Pentecost, Year A)

We Make Known God's Deeds

(Psalm 105:1-6)

Left Side: We give thanks to God, we call on the name of the LORD, we make known God's deeds among the peoples.

*Right Side: We sing to God, sing praises to God;
we tell of all the LORD'S wonderful works.*

Left Side: We glory in God's holy name; let the hearts of those who seek the LORD rejoice.

*Right Side: We seek the LORD and the LORD'S strength;
we seek God's presence continually.*

Left Side: We remember the wonderful works God has done, God's miracles, and God's judgments.

*Right Side: We are offspring of God's servant Abraham, children of Jacob,
God's chosen ones.*

All: We give thanks to the LORD, we call on God's name, we make known God's deeds among the peoples.

(Tony Peterson, Twelfth Sunday after Pentecost, Year A)

Thank You Jesus, Thank You Lord

(Psalm 105:1-6, 23-26, 45c)

One: O give thanks to the Lord.
Many: Thank you Jesus! Thank you Lord!

One: O give thanks to the Lord.
Many: Thank you for raising prophets like Moses, Martin and Mandela.

One: O give thanks to the Lord.
Many: Thank you for putting fire in the mouth of "everyday prophets" who speak truth to power.

One: O give thanks to the Lord.
Many: Thank you for ignoring our excuses and inspiring us to carry out your prophetic will.

One: O give thanks to the Lord.
Many: Thank you that some "Moses" is among us to speak for the oppressed. A Moses who just might be me.

(Kwasi I. Kena, Thirteenth Sunday after Pentecost, Year A)

It Is Truly Wonderful when Relatives Live Together in Peace

(Psalm 133, CEV, TNIV, NRSV)

Speaker 1: It is truly wonderful when relatives live together in peace.
People: It is like the dew falling on mountains, where the LORD has promised to bless his people with life forevermore.

Speaker 2: How good and pleasant it is when God's people live together in unity!
People: It is as if the dew were falling on God's mountain.

Speaker 3: For there the LORD bestows his blessing, even life forevermore.
People: How very good and pleasant it is when kindred live together in unity!

All: It is like the dew that falls on the mountains, for there the LORD ordained his blessing, life for evermore.

(Tony Peterson, Thirteenth Sunday after Pentecost, Year A)

The Triune God Is Here and Dwells in This Place

One: The Spirit of God is here and dwells in this place.
Many: We are spiritually alive and our faith is well.

One: The Spirit of the Son is here and dwells in this place.
Many: Our worship is active and alive.

One: The Holy Spirit is here and dwells in this place.
Many: God is here, Creator, Savior, and Spirit.

One: Let us greet this Great God with our hymn of praise.

(Eugene Blair, Sixteenth Sunday after Pentecost, Year A)

Go before Us, O God, and We Will Worship

One: This week it felt like life was pursuing us, like Pharaoh's pursuing army.
Many: Go before us, O God, like a pillar of cloud to show us the way.

One: Sometimes life feels hopeless, like being pursued by Pharaoh's army.
Many: Go before us, O God, like a pillar of fire to light the way.

One: Let us worship this God who goes before us day and night.
Many: Let us worship God with our praises, our hymns, and our offerings.

(Eugene Blair, Seventeenth Sunday after Pentecost, Year A)

Come, All You People, and Give Thanks

One: Come all you people and give thanks to the Lord.
Many: Come, let us call upon the name of the Lord.

One: Sing psalms to God and speak of God's wondrous works.
Many: Our hearts rejoice. We glory in the Lord.

One: Seek the face of the Lord forevermore.
Many: Let us recall the works, the wonders, and the judgments of the Lord.

One: Come, let us greet this great God with our hymn of praise.

(Eugene Blair Eighteenth Sunday after Pentecost, Year A)

Let Us Worship the One Who Gives Us Strength

One: It has been a long week. We are tired and wearied by the journey.
Many: Come, let us sit with one another in prayer, praise, and song.

One: Jesus said to come to him when we were weary and heavy laden.
Many: Come, let the saints of God lift their weary, drooping hands in praise and thanksgiving.

One: Jesus said he is the way, the truth, and the life.
Many: Come, let us worship the one who gives us strength.

(Eugene Blair, Nineteenth Sunday after Pentecost, Year A)

We Your Children, Acknowledge this Morning that You Alone Are God"

(Exodus 32:1-14)

Gracious God, You are an awesome God! You are powerful, excellent and faithful. Your love is too great to measure. We, your children, acknowledge this morning that you alone are God. No idols or gods are welcome here. Only you. We love and adore you! You are worthy of our praise! Come, be with us your people this day. We hunger for your presence–in Jesus' name, amen.

(Lillian C. Smith, Twenty-first Sunday after Pentecost, Year A)

"The Lord Reigns, Holy"

(Adapted from Psalm 99, NRSV)

One: The LORD Reigns!
Many Let the people tremble!

One: The LORD is great in Zion; the LORD is exalted over all the peoples.
Many: Let the people praise your great and awesome name! Holy are you LORD!

One: Our God is a mighty and just God!
Many: Extol the LORD our God; worship at God's footstool.

All: Holy is the LORD!

(Lillian C. Smith, Twenty-second Sunday after Pentecost, Year A)

The Promises of God Are Not Always Fulfilled in Our Lifetime

The promises of God are not always fulfilled in our lifetime. Moses saw the Promised Land, but did not enter into it. Many of our enslaved ancestors received the promise of freedom and abundant life, but did not experience it. We are living out that promise made to them. We live out promises made to saints who have gone before us. We are both living God's promise and awaiting the fulfillment of God's promise. Times may be hard. We may cry sometimes. Justice may seem to tarry. Yet, God remains faithful and God's promises are true! Let us worship God! Amen.

(Lillian C. Smith, Twenty-third Sunday after Pentecost, Year A)

You Have Been Our Dwelling Place in All Generations

(Psalm 90:1-4, 16-17a)

One suggestion is to have a youth/young adult liturgical dancer/or the dance team choreograph movements to this text.

One: Lord, you have been our dwelling place in all generations.
Many: Before the mountains were brought forth, or ever you had formed the earth and the world, from everlasting to everlasting you are God.

One: You turn us back to dust and say, "Turn back, you mortals."
Many: For a thousand years in your sight are like yesterday when it is past, or like a watch in the night.

One: Let your work be manifest to your servants, and your glorious power to their children.
Many: Let the favor of the Lord our God be upon us and prosper the work of our hands!

(Lillian C. Smith, Twenty-third Sunday after Pentecost, Year A)

God Let Us Count the Ways You Never Leave Us

Morning Prayer

(Unison) God, let us count the ways you never leave us. Your Light of Day greeted us this morning. The smell of life filled our nostrils with the crisp, chilly air of a new day. The melody of gently crackling leaves whispered your love in our ears. These are among the Good Morning gifts we thank you for. You have given us another day in your Precious Presence.

Come what may this day: angry traffic, angry words, paved roads, paved ways, we will praise your Holy Name! And so we greet you this day with shouts of joy and thanksgiving. Amen.

(Sherrie Dobbs Johnson, Twenty-fourth Sunday after Pentecost, Year A)

How Many of Us

Gathering Call

One: How many of you feel, sometimes, that The Wrong is just too strong for you to handle, and you sink into deep despair and sleepless nights? Or, that we fight Wrong with rage? Unable to pull in our anger, we spew it on those who wronged us. If this is you, just bow your head. My head is bowed. *(Leader bows head.)*
(People's Response: bow your head.)

One: How many of us have tried our best and gotten nowhere fast? Then, we decided to "Let go," and let the Lord fight our battles? If this is you, just raise your right hand and say, "Amen." *(Leader raises right hand and says Amen!)*
(People's Response: raise right hand and say "Amen.")

One: How many of you come here today to witness to the fact that God never leaves us alone?–that because of Jesus, we still have favor with God? So we'll go where God tells us to go and do what God tells us to do. If this is you, just raise your left hand and say, "We thank you Lord Jesus!" "We praise you Lord Jesus!" *(Leader raises left hand.)*
(People's Response: raise left hand.)

One: How many of you come here today believing that you can fly, knowing that because of Jesus, we can soar. If this is you, raise both hands to a Mighty Good God and say "Hallelujah!" *(Leader does the same.)*

(Sherrie Dobbs Johnson, Twenty-fourth Sunday after Pentecost, Year A)

And Still We Made It

(Unison) Lord, we thank you that we did not miss our blessing today. Heads to comb, socks to match, and still we made it. Discouragements and disruptions, and still we made it! Burnt toast or no toast, but still we made it. Wrinkled clothes or pressed clothes, but still we made it. So glad to be in your presence one more time! Amen.

(Sherrie Dobbs Johnson, Twenty-fifth Sunday after Pentecost, Year A)

We Come This Morning Seeking

One: We come this morning seeking healing, so we bring you our pain.
Many: We come this morning seeking answers, so we bring you our questions.

One: We come this morning seeking comfort, so we bring you our dis-ease.
Many: We come this morning seeking freedom, so we bring you our inhibitions.

One: We come this morning seeking peace, so we bring you our conflicts.
Many: We come this morning seeking love, so we bring you our pride.

One: We come this morning seeking forgiveness, so we bring you our sins.
Many: We come this morning seeking success, so we bring you our fear.

All: We come to you, O God, who makes a way out of no way. We come seeking to be in your presence one more time. Take away our sadness and give us your joy.

(Sherrie Dobbs Johnson, Twenty-sixth Sunday after Pentecost, Year A)

We Thank You for Believing in Us

(Unison) Lord, we thank you for believing in us. Every time we take one step, you take two. We ask for cloudless days, you beam down sunshine. We ask for mercy, you shower us with love. We ask for success, you crown us with victory. Your love is too great for us to understand. Double our faith; double our courage; double our praise! Amen.

(Sherrie Dobbs Johnson, Twenty-sixth Sunday after Pentecost, Year A)

You Believe in Us More than We Believe in Ourselves

Creator God, we come into the world with nothing, but all we have comes from you. Over and over again, when we've taken one step toward you, you've taken two toward us. When we've given up the little we have, you've supplied us more than we can use. When we've doubted but forged on anyway, you turned our fledgling steps into flight. When we've been ready to shed our doubts, you've dressed us in the courage of Deborah. When we've been ready to shed our ignorance, you've planted in us the wisdom of Deborah.

You believe in us more than we believe in ourselves. You believe in us even when our belief in you is shallow. Thank you for investing in this risky venture called humanity. Thank you for investing in us. You are a God who specializes in "insider-trading," and we thank you for that. Amen.

(Sherrie Dobbs Johnson, Twenty-sixth Sunday after Pentecost, Year A)

Make a Joyful Noise

One: Make a joyful noise unto the Lord!
Many: (sung #95, *UMH*) Doxology

One: Make a joyful noise unto the Lord!
Many: (sung #94, *UMH*) Doxology (Alternate Tune)

One: Worship the Lord with gladness: come into his presence with singing!
Many: (sung #99, *UMH*, verse one) To God Be the Glory

One: (Read Psalm 100)

(Sherrie Dobbs Johnson, Christ the King Sunday/Sunday before Thanksgiving, Year A)

Congregational Prayers

Gracious God, Let Your Kingdom Come

Gracious God, let your kingdom come.
We know we war against your kingdom—
At school, we drop hate bombs on the girl who is different.
At home, we slice our family with our tongues.
At work, we stab our friends with rumors we spread.
Even at church, we find enemies and attack.
But your kingdom can be on earth,
We can experience the fullness of your glory—
If we release our weapons.
Help us, Lord, to study war no more.
In the name of Jesus, Amen.

(Ciona D. Rouse, First Sunday in Advent, Year A)

Your Glory Paints Itself All over the Earth's Canvas

Wonder-working God, blessed Savior, your glory paints itself all over the earth's canvas. But we know needy children. We know cruel terrorists pointing guns on our streets and planting bombs in our buildings. We know injustice that keeps the poor from standing. They all seem to rest in the shadows. But we also know your redemptive waters. We know that baptism with you means we live into your glory. And we know that you are coming again. Help us, Lord, paint the tough places beautiful with your love as we prepare the world for you to come. Amen.

(Ciona D. Rouse, Second Sunday in Advent, Year A)

On that Glorious Day

One: Jesus Christ, the King of all Kings, was born on that glorious day in the most humble of ways –
Many: Wrapped in pieces of cloth,
Surrounded by donkeys and sheep,
Placed in a trough where animals feasted,
Our invisible God was given a face—
A tiny, precious, beautiful baby clothed in humility!
We are made in your image, God.
Remind us of the humble ways you reveal yourself
Through Jesus who entered our world,
Walked on this earth,
Died on the Cross,
And manifested your glory
Through the Resurrection! Amen.

(Ciona D. Rouse, Fourth Sunday in Advent, Year A)

Come, Lord Jesus, with Justice for the Earth

Behold the Lord, God's Servant, the Chosen One.
God's Spirit rests upon the Son to bring justice to the nations.
We need justice in our homes and communities today.
Come, Lord Jesus, with justice for the earth.

We need justice in our schools and on our streets today.
We need justice in our nations and world today.
Come, Lord Jesus, with justice for the earth.

Lord, God's Servant, the Chosen One,
We call upon you to uproot ungodliness
In every crevice of human existence today.
Come, Lord Jesus, with justice for the earth.

We call upon you Lord, the only Righteous Judge,
To dispense the type of justice that transforms illicit behavior.
Come, Lord Jesus, with justice for the earth.

We call upon you, Lord, to provide the kind of justice
That clears muddy waters of corruption.
Come, Lord Jesus, with justice for the earth.

The earth cries with the voices of the hungry,
The maimed and the slaughtered innocents.
Come, Lord Jesus, with justice for the earth.

(Kwasi I. Kena, Baptism of the Lord, Year A)

For the Revelation of Your Mystery in Jesus Christ

(Ephesians 3:1-12)

Gracious, Giving God,

We give thanks to you for the revelation of your mystery in Jesus Christ to all humanity. We are privileged to be of this generation who knows your love come down in flesh. How the ancestors longed for our time! How the prophets hoped for it! In past generations, we gentiles were not a part of this commonwealth of hope; but now in Christ, you have brought us near. Thank you. Bless you for the gift of your grace that works powerfully in us, your people, your church. Thank you for this never ending richness of Christ that gives our lives the wealth of your presence. Your eternal purpose has been carried out in Christ Jesus, and you have called us to serve that purpose with joy and commitment. Help us to be bold and confident in faith; help us to trust you fully and to walk in this grace and to share gladly the revelation of your mystery that now belongs to us. In the name of Christ we pray, amen.

(Valerie Bridgeman Davis, Epiphany, Years A, B, and C)

Shine Brightly on Us

(Psalm 27, Isaiah 9:1-4)

Guide our feet Lord. Show us the light of grace when we would judge others too harshly. Warm our hearts with the glow of your love when we would spew icy words of spite. Illumine our souls with joyful delight when sadness tries to take over the day. Shine brightly on us today, Lord, until we reflect your glory as a witness to this world. Amen.

(Kwasi I. Kena, Third Sunday after Epiphany, Year A)

Prayers of the People

(1 Corinthians 1:10-18)

God of Unity,

We come before you dismayed at our own divisions. We have struggled as your church to live in unity; but we are divided–along all the fault lines of our societies. The ruptures in our families, among friends, among denominations, among nations are wide and deep. When we attempt to get on the same page, we build taller walls and dig deeper trenches. God, help us! We know that Christ is not divided. We know that it is your baptism to which we have been called. It is your service to which we are compelled. You have called us to proclaim the gospel, but we even fight about what that is. Help us, God! Help us to give up our power, and our privileges. Help us to yield for the sake and cause of the cross of Jesus. Help us to want the unity you share, for you are one; in you there is no division. Help us to embrace and to live the foolishness of a life emptied of power and given to service, in the likeness of our Savior, Jesus Christ. Help us to walk in salvation–in the name of the Servant Christ, amen.

(Valerie Bridgeman Davis, Third Sunday after Epiphany, Year A)

Give Us an Eye

(Micah 6:8)

(Unison) Give us, O Lord, an eye for injustice–for it is only when are able to recognize injustice and feel its awful sting that we will be moved to make things right.

Give us, O Lord, a tender heart–sometimes we are too hardhearted to recognize when we have been uncaring, unfeeling, or unkind.

Give us, O Lord, the ability to view life from the dust–all our lives we have been taught to make others proud, to be proud of ourselves, to hold our heads high, all the while missing the virtues of being poor in spirit.

Teach us, dear Lord, to do justice, love kindness, and to walk humbly with you. Amen.

(Carolyn W. Dandridge, Fourth Sunday after Epiphany, Year A)

Transform Us into Prophetic People

(To be read by three youth.)

Youth 1: When Jesus appeared to his disciples on the mountain of transfiguration,
They realized that he was "that special one."
Change us, too, Lord, into "somebody special."
Change our hearts until they beam like the sun.
Change our lives into shining examples of your grace.

All: Transform us into prophetic people of God moved by the Holy Spirit.

Youth 2: Give us a "spirit" so unique that no one can match it,
An essence so mysterious that no artist can catch it.
We want to live in the strength that lies deep within our souls.
We long for an appearance that reveals character,
And a strong determination to follow your will.

All: Transform us into prophetic people of God moved by the Holy Spirit.

Youth 3: Give us powerful arms and strong legs
For the burdens that lie ahead
Give us eyes for the truth,
And a mind that stays on you.
We want to be like that perfect one, "that special one."

Youth 1, 2, and 3: Transform us, too! That's why we call on you!

All: Transform us into prophetic people of God moved by the Holy Spirit.

(Catrinia N. Harrison & Carolyn W. Dandridge, Transfiguration Sunday, Year A)

Prayer of Thanksgiving

Almighty Great I Am,
We thank you for opportunities to praise and magnify your goodness.
We thank you for your son Jesus who sacrificially gave his life up for us.
We thank you for power that lifts us from the depths of pain and sorrow.
We thank you for rainbows that shine through storms of war-torn countries.
We thank you for people who seek cures for diseases with names and diseases yet
to come.

We thank you for stones that provide a hiding place as we climb the mountain of life.
We seek to know you better.
We are mindful of the praise and glory that belong to you.
We are conscious that you are a loving and forgiving Creator.
We are thankful that you bless us each day with your goodness and mercy.
We know that all things work together for the good of those who know you and who seek you. Hear our prayer in the name of Jesus the King of Kings. Amen.

(Carolyn W. Dandridge, General, Year A)

Lord, Here I Am

(For one reader and congregation or multiple readers and congregation.)

Now Abraham was the first to go and must have been a brave man.
Because you did not say where he was going
and still he followed your command.
He shows us that when you ask us to move, we should say:
Lord, here I am.

There are many who are bold,
and, in your name, take a stand
when your people are hurting each other in ways we can't comprehend.
Without a moment's hesitation, they say to you:
Lord, here I am.

When we hear tales of injustice and oppression
happening across your vast land
we believe you want us to respond–to be your feet, to be your hands.
And while I don't know the work you need me to do:
Lord, here I am.

You are working through our lives
to fulfill your mighty will and plan
And it requires a submission we sometimes cannot understand.
But as you promised to never forsake us, we each say:
Lord, here I am.

(Ciona D. Rouse, Second Sunday in Lent, Year A)

I Can't Imagine

(Divide reading between the left and the right sides of the congregation.)

**Left: I can't imagine being an Israelite
crying, "Hallelujah!" for freedom
while being uncertain of God's great plan.**

Right: But I know how to thank God for salvation
even when I am anxious about what will greet me each new day.

**Left: I can't imagine being thirsty in the desert
and seeing only sand and stones and dryness
everywhere except for my tears.**

Right: But I know what it means to cry long and hard
because life seems very empty and dry.

**Left: I can't imagine following Moses
on a long path
and not always trusting that he knew the way.**

Right: But I know what it means
to doubt that my leaders, my friends, or my family are doing what is best.

**Left: And I can't imagine the miracle
of drinking refreshing water from a hard rock
when hope seemed too far away.**

Right: But I know what it means
to feel your blessings pour upon me in the deepest times of despair.

**Left: Lord, I can't always imagine the stories in your Word,
because I never walked the same paths as the Israelites.**

Right: But I know your Word speaks to my life today,
and I praise you for being that water from the rock.

(Ciona D. Rouse, Third Sunday in Lent, Year A)

Triumphal Entry

Today, God, we rejoice with Christians everywhere that there was at least one day when Jesus received the recognition he deserved. We rejoice, knowing that his triumphal entry means that truth cannot remain hidden and that good hearts everywhere recognize truth when it appears. We stand in hope with people on many continents, in many circumstances who are waiting for the day when their truth can be told. We stand with them in faith knowing that the same God who could have commanded the rocks to shout truth in Jerusalem will not allow truth to be suppressed and good people to be crushed forever. Amen.

(Safiyah Fosua, Palm Sunday, Year A)

In the Name and Pain of the Crucified One

Faithful God, we stand in the dim shadows of a cross, longing for resurrection. But today we pause to remember the pain of the cross, and the pain of the crosses we've faced. We pause to cry for the Sudan, for Rwanda, for more than one-thirds of the African continent suffering from full-blown AIDS. As the disciples wept on that fateful day so long ago, we weep for the savior and for the tree, and all the trees that one represented, from which he hung. We cry for our ecology: birds slick from oil, forests decimated causing mudslides and runoff, air polluted from our disdain for the creation that cries with us. As those first disciples wondered whether that fateful day was the end of their dreams, we admit we are afraid that our dream of a just, nonviolent world is fleeting and in peril of death. Help us God as we live in the tension between this death and your seeming silence, the time after the crucifixion and before the resurrection—in the name and pain of the Crucified One, amen.

(Valerie Bridgeman Davis, Good Friday, Year A)

We Are Helpless without You

Great God, our Creator, we are helpless without you. We can't protect ourselves from danger, nor can we will our hearts to sing. You gave us Jesus, who has built us up and surrounded us with his grace. When we think of our lives before Jesus entered in, we must confess that we were as cold tombs. Now, we dwell in the sunshine of your love under the mighty sky of faith. We've come to enjoy each other and communion with your Holy Spirit. Let your goodness and mercy follow us all the days of our lives, and may we dwell in your house forever! Amen.

(Sherrie Dobbs Johnson, Fourth Sunday of Easter, Year A)

Teach Us Not To Despise Small Things

(Unison Prayer)

O God, teach us not to despise small things.
Remind us that the kingdom of heaven is like a tiny mustard seed.
Turn our attention to the small things that bless others.
You have planted seeds of great potential in our souls
Help us develop our potential so that you and others can depend on it.
Turn our attention to what is small but potent.
O God, you have entrusted us with gifts and graces that can bless many people.
Help us not to overlook the smallest ability.
O God, you have placed the destiny of the kingdom of heaven inside of us.
Turn our attention to the small things that this congregation can do to make a tremendous difference in human lives. Amen.

(Kwasi I. Kena, Tenth Sunday after Pentecost, Year A)

Lord If It's You…

(Matthew 14:22-33)

Lord, if it's you, we need to hear from you

When we are alone
When we go away to pray
When we have little faith
When we are battered by the waves
When the wind is against us
When we get in the boat
When we're terrified by our ghosts
When we seek you on the mountain
When we cry out in fear
When we start walking on water
When we begin to sink
When we are far from land

Lord, if it's you,
speak to us,
calm our fears,
calm our storms
Strengthen our resolve
Remind us who you are
Walk to us
Call to us
Save us
Reach out your hand and catch us
Quiet the wind around us

Lord, if it's you, we worship you for "Truly you are the Son of God."

(Tony Peterson, Twelfth Sunday after Pentecost, Year A)

Lord, Free Your People from False Beliefs
(A Pastoral Prayer)

Lord, free your people from false beliefs.

Free your people from the false belief that *you love some of us more than others.*
That if someone has more or better "stuff," like:
money
family
health
ease
peace and quiet
comfort
it's because you love that person more.

Free your people from the false belief *that we are defective beyond repair.*
That you are waiting for an opportunity to punish us . . .
That you don't care about sinners . . .
That you can't see past our sin to love us.

Free your people from the false belief *that suffering cannot be redemptive*
That we only suffer because we did something wrong.

Free your people from the false belief *that we've been good long enough.*
That what we do in private doesn't matter . . .
That following Jesus is nothing if it doesn't make us feel better . . .
That we deserve to indulge ourselves.

Free your people from the false belief *that celebrity is better than salvation*
That high-profile Christians are better at following Jesus . . .
That those who do not agree with Christians in the media are not good
Christians.

Free your people from the false belief that *we can get along fine without you.*

Free us from the false beliefs that hold us captive and teach us
That you love us all,
No one is beyond repair,
Sometimes, even good people suffer,
You love those who follow righteousness,
You alone are our salvation,
And that each of us needs you. Amen.

(Tony Peterson, Fifteenth Sunday after Pentecost, Year A)

We Give You Thanks

We give you thanks O LORD, we call on your name. We will make known your deeds among the peoples.

We'll sing to you, we'll sing praises to you; we'll tell of all your wonderful works. We glory in your holy name; let the hearts of those who seek you rejoice.

We seek you, LORD, and your strength; and your presence continually. We remember the wonderful works you have done, your miracles, and the judgments you uttered.

You are the LORD our God; your judgments are in all the earth.

Amen and Amen.

(Tony Peterson, Fifteenth Sunday after Pentecost, Year A)

Litanies

When Mary's Baby Was Born

When Mary's baby was born . . .
Calendars were renumbered
  The heavens applauded
  And a new star appeared in the sky.

The angels sang,
  And shepherds came running into town.

Inquiring wise men brought gifts and unwittingly
  Frightened King Herod when Mary's baby was born.

When Mary's baby walked this earth . . .
People came from miles around to sit at his feet
  And hear the wisdom that could only come from God.

They brought the sick, the lame,
  And those who were troubled
    In their minds.

The winds and the seas had to obey him
  Because he was Emmanuel, God with us.

Formidable demons trembled
  And ran away screaming
    When Mary's baby walked upon this earth.

When Mary's baby died . . .
Even the earth was grieved,
  The sun hid its face and refused to shine,
   And the ground staggered and lost its footing
   (Some called it an earthquake.)

 Graves opened up and saints walked around
  While Roman soldiers
   Confessed that Mary's baby, Jesus, was the Son of God.

But now,
 Mary's baby lives again

  And is seated in heaven.

Mary's baby lives again

  And is praying for you.

Mary's baby lives again

And makes it possible for you to have joy.

(Safiyah Fosua, Advent Season, Year A)

Wake Up!

Wake up! Today is a new day.
Arise! The moment is now. God's grace is here. And God's kingdom draws nearer.
Wake up! Get ready for a new way to live.
We slept for so long, pretending to know you. But we neglected to worship you
with whole hearts. We walked past you when you were the blind man on the cor-
ner, stepped over you when you were afflicted.
Wake up! We can start again.
Your grace is sufficient, Lord. We do not have to be silent in the face of injustice.
We don't have to accept what the world calls living. We can arise!
Wake up! Live for Jesus!
We will clothe you, feed you, welcome you and love you, Lord.
Wake up! God is creating something new in us. Wake up!

(Ciona D. Rouse, First Sunday in Advent, Year A)

Oh, Zion! We sing of Zion!

(Suggestion: Have a youth or young adult and an elder lead this litany.)

First One: There is a street, the Sacred Way, where the road is safe and spotless.
When we're marching to Zion, beautiful Zion

Second One: There are no pickpockets. There is no vandalism.
Oh, Zion! We sing of Zion!

First One: You hear no obscenities. There is no harm, no rebellion.
When we're marching to Zion, beautiful Zion

Second One: No need to hold your purse, to hold your loved one's hand, or to hold your breath in fear.
Oh, Zion! We sing of Zion!

First One: There are no illegal goods sold on the corner.
When we're marching to Zion, beautiful Zion

Second One: There are no tragic accidents, no death at all.
Oh, Zion! We sing of Zion!

First One: No need to ask for directions; even the most foolish can find their way.
When we're marching to Zion, beautiful Zion

Second One: It is a road for the redeemed! And we will walk this road with Christ, the King!
All: Amen! Amen! Amen!

(Ciona D. Rouse, Third Sunday in Advent, Year A)

Save Us Jesus, Save Us Lord

(Refrain sung to same tune as response of "Send Me, Lord"
#497 The United Methodist Hymnal)

Jesus said, "Come to me all you who are weary," weary of spending more money than you have, weary of running out of things to want, weary of feeling no joy, no excitement.
Sung Refrain: Save us Jesus, save us Jesus. Save us Jesus, save us Lord.

Jesus said, "Come to me all you who are weary," weary of not having enough, weary of being not good enough, weary of being taken for granted, being lonely, being sick, being abused.
Sung Refrain: Save us Jesus, save us Jesus. Save us Jesus, save us Lord.

Jesus said, "Come to me all you are weary," weary of being oppressed and oppressing, weary of tasting death because of violence, because of war, weary of being violent, weary of being warriors.
Sung Refrain: Save us Jesus, save us Jesus. Save us Jesus, save us Lord.

Come Jesus Christ into our lives this Advent season, give us rest, give us peace, and save us.
Sung Refrain: Save us Jesus, save us Jesus. Save us Jesus, save us Lord.

(Sherrie Dobbs Johnson, Advent, Year A)

Like A Shoot Out of a Stump

(Isaiah 11:1-10)

Cut off from home and heritage, cut down to build somebody else's prosperity, Lord we come.

Cut off from songs, traditions, and culture that kept us together so long, Lord we come.

Cut off by a world that expects more misery and more money, Lord we come.

Cut off by systems that delight in evil and ignore righteousness, Lord we come.

But because we serve God who judges people like us with righteousness, God will send a righteous judge, like a shoot out of a stump.

Because God is with us, the wolf will dwell with the lamb, like a shoot out of a stump.

Let your spirit of wisdom and understanding rise up in us, like a shoot out of a stump.

We expect you to help us grow powerful and united, righteous and holy, even in a sinful world, like a root out of a stump.

(Tim Warner, Second Sunday in Advent, Year A)

Roll, Jordan, Roll
(Deep Repentance, Sweet Salvation)

(May be used as a choral litany sung to the tune of
"Swing Low, Sweet Chariot" #703, The United Methodist Hymnal)

Deep repentance, sweet salvation
Roll, Jordan, roll
Sweet waters, deep river
Roll, Jordan, roll

Step to the shores just as I am
Roll, Jordan, roll
The waters will wash away my sins
Roll, Jordan, roll
Dirt off my shoulder, soil off my shoes
Roll, Jordan, roll
To cleanse my soul for the Good News!
Roll, Jordan, roll
Not just my skin, Lord, cleanse my heart
Roll, Jordan, roll
Take all of me and make a new start
Roll, Jordan, roll
I'll leave these waters changed and clean
Roll, Jordan, roll
to live a life with the King!
Roll, Jordan, roll

Deep repentance, sweet salvation
Roll, Jordan, roll
Sweet waters, deep river
Roll, Jordan, roll

(Ciona D. Rouse, Second Sunday of Advent, Year A)

Glory to the King

Jesus Christ, the same yesterday, today, and forever, has come!
All honor and glory to the King of kings!

He came to a teenaged mother Mary and an adopted father Joseph, humbly, on a glorious night.
Glory to the newborn king!

He came with good news that God loves us all, radically and boldly.

He will cover a sinful world with blankets of salvation, wiping our criminal records clean.
Glory to the saving king!

He comes lovingly when neighbors knock on our doors asking for help, looking for hope. He comes when we are tempted to close the door.
Glory to the compassionate king!

He will come again to us who are adopted into God's reign, fulfilling a promise not to abandon us to an orphanage of sin and death.
Glory to the promise-keeping king!

Jesus Christ, the same yesterday, today, and forever is coming!
All honor and glory to the King of kings!

(Ciona D. Rouse, Advent, Year A)

Revealed by Any Means Necessary

(Philippians 2:5-11)

Lord, you have never been ashamed to reveal your love–
By any means necessary.

You emptied yourself and took the form of a slave–for us
You suffered under oppressive rulers and powers–for us
You humbled yourself and became obedient to death on a cross–for us

Lord, you revealed yourself in human form
So that we could "see" what God is like.

Lord, reveal yourself to us today–by any means necessary.

Even if it means asking us to endure suffering for your sake
Even if it means asking us to go out of our way to help a stranger

Lord, reveal yourself to us today–by any means necessary.

Even if it means asking us to give away what we "thought" we had to
have
Even if it means asking us to deny ourselves for the sake of others

Lord, reveal yourself to us today–by any means necessary.

Lord, reveal yourself to us today
So that we may reveal your love to others–by any means necessary!

(Kwasi I. Kena, Epiphany Sunday, Year A)

Lord, I Want To Be a Christian

(*Sing*) Lord, I want to be a Christian in my heart, in my heart.
Lord, I want to be a Christian in my heart.
You alone can change me, Lord.
Wash me in the waters of baptism that I may become a new person.

Wash away everything that stands between me and your holiness.

(*Sing*) In my heart, in my heart.
Lord, I want to be a Christian in my heart.
You alone can change me, Lord.
Wash away this temper that gets me into more trouble than I can handle.
Wash away the massive wants that place me in constant financial jeopardy.

(*Sing*) In my heart, in my heart.
Lord, I want to be a Christian in my heart.
You alone can change me, Lord.
Wash away my envy that separates me from the people I should love.
Wash away everything that stands between me and your holiness.

(*Sing*) In my heart, in my heart.
Lord, I want to be a Christian in my heart.
You alone can change me, Lord.
Wash me with your cleansing power that I may be a child of God.
You alone can change me, Lord.

(*Sing*) Lord, I want to be a Christian in my heart in my heart.
Lord, I want to be a Christian in my heart.

(Kwasi I. Kena, Baptism of the Lord, Year A)

Lamb of God, Who Takes Away the Sin
(John 1:29-42)

Sing refrain of "Lamb of God," ***The Faith We Sing,*** **2113**

Here is the Lamb of God who takes away the sin of the world.
Your sin and my sin and the sin of our enemies–

Here is the Lamb of God who takes away the sin of the world
The Spirit descended upon Him from heaven like a dove

Here is the Lamb of God who takes away the sin of the world.
John the Baptist testified of him saying, "This is the Son of God."

Sing refrain of "Lamb of God," ***The Faith We Sing,*** **2113**

Here is the Lamb of God who takes away the sin of the world.
Disciples followed him, listened to him, and learned from him.
Here is the Lamb of God who takes away the sin of the world.
People rushed to tell others, "We have found the Messiah."
Here is the Lamb of God who takes away the sin of the world.
Your sin and my sin and the sin of our enemies

Sing refrain of "Lamb of God," ***The Faith We Sing,*** **2113**
(Optional: Sing the entire hymn.)

(Kwasi I. Kena, Second Sunday after Epiphany, Year A)

The Lord Is My Light

(Psalm 27)

My world is full of fear-filled intrusions.
Just walking down my street is a daily test of nerve.
The other day I saw the chalk outline of what used to be a living soul.
What word do you have for me?

Sing verse one of "The Lord Is My Light," #160 *African American Heritage Hymnal*

I heard the sharp "pop, pop, pop" of bullets piercing the air last night.
The local news pieced together the story of another lost life.
Some days I just turn down the sound and wait for the sports.
What word do you have for me?

Sing verse two of "The Lord Is My Light," #160 *African American Heritage Hymnal*

When his fist ignores her humanity and
Her voice dismantles his manhood and
Their defiance embarrasses their parents
What word do you have for us?

Sing verse three of "The Lord Is My Light," #160 *African American Heritage Hymnal*

All: Lord, today is the day that we'll see your Light
Today is the day that our souls will be convinced of your Salvation
Today is the day that this church will reflect your Light and your Salvation
To hurting families and suffering communities!

Sing verse one and the refrain of "The Lord Is My Light," #160 *African American Heritage Hymnal*

(Kwasi I. Kena, Third Sunday after Epiphany, Year A)

What Is Truth?

(John 18:1-19:42)

One: When Jesus finished praying in the garden, he went to meet his future–a certain death, a certain betrayal
Many: All around Jesus, people ask "what is truth."

One: He was met by soldiers and false accusers
Many: All around Jesus, people ask "what is truth."

One: Judas kissed away the meals and the miles they had shared together
Many: All around Jesus, people ask "what is truth."

One: Peter tried to protect him from an inevitable and foretold end
Many: All around Jesus, people ask "what is truth."

One: When he couldn't protect him, Peter's fear led him to deny him
Many: All around Jesus, people ask "what is truth."

One: From hall to hall and heart to heart, they led him the dark of night to broken justice and false witnesses
Many: All around Jesus, people ask "what is truth."

One: Pilate questioned his statement: "I came to testify to the truth," I came to be on the side of truth
Many: All around Jesus, people ask "what is truth."

One: What was Pilate to do since he saw the truth with his eyes, but did not have courage to free it?
Many: All around Jesus, people ask "what is truth."

One: Crucify him still rings across time, because truth unrecognized always goes punished
Many: And still we're asking, "What is truth."

(Valerie Bridgeman Davis, Good Friday, Years ABC)

God's Loving Mercy Endures Forever

(Psalm 118:1-6)

Many: Give thanks to the LORD, for God is good; God's love endures forever.
One: Let the people of God say: God's love endures forever

Many: Let the priests who serve in prayer say: God's mercy endures forever
One: Let all who reverence the Creating God say: God's mercy endures forever!

Many: We know what it is to cry out in anguish and fear
One: God's loving mercy endures forever

Many: God is with us; we will not be afraid
One: Let all who reverence the Saving God say: God's loving mercy endures forever!

Many: The LORD is our help and refuge; God's loving mercy endures forever
One: We put our hope in God rather than governments

All: Oh, Give thanks to the LORD, for God's loving mercy endures forever.

(Valerie Bridgeman Davis, Lenten Season, Easter Day, Years ABC)

Enter In and Shout About It

(Psalm 118:19-29)

(This litany may be divided and used in separate sections of the worship.)

One: Open the gates of righteous
Many: Enter in and give thanks to the Lord

One: This is the gate of God
Many: Enter in and be saved!

One: This is the gate of God
Many: Give thanks as you enter in

One: This is the place where God answers
Many: Enter in and give thanks to the Lord for salvation!

One: The stone the builders rejected is the strongest part of God's house
Many: Jesus is that stone; give thanks as you enter in

One: The stone that was rejected is our Rock and strength
Many: The Lord has made it so, and it is marvelous in our eyes

One: This is the day the Lord has made
Many: We rejoice, glad in it!

One: This is the day the Lord has made
Many: We came to shout about it!

One: God is our salvation and our success
Many: We came to shout about it!

One: Blessed is the One who comes in the name of God
Many: We came to shout about it!

One: From God's sanctuary we bless you
Many: We came to shout about it!

One: The Lord is God and shines on us
Many: We came to shout about it!

One: We join the festive procession from age to age and place to place
Many: Give thanks to the Lord, for God is good.

All: God's love endures forever and we came to shout about it!

(Valerie Bridgeman Davis, Passion/Palm Sunday, Years A, B, C)

It Is Impossible for Death to Hold Us

(Acts 2:14a, 22-32)

One: Ever felt abandoned to the grave? Left to languish in places and situations that did not speak life?
Many: It was impossible for death to hold Jesus; it's impossible for death to hold us.

One: In the face of poverty and lack, in the face of unjust governmental systems and religious institutions that don't respond:
Many: It was impossible for death to hold Jesus; it's impossible for death to hold us.

One: In the face of sadness as disease, death, and hopelessness threaten our very existence
Many: It was impossible for death to hold Jesus; it's impossible for death to hold us.

One: Where is the voice of the prophet? Where is the call to hope?
Many: This is our prophetic hope: It was impossible for death to hold Jesus; it's impossible for death to hold us.

(Valerie Bridgeman Davis, Second Sunday of Easter, Year A)

Anybody Here?

(Psalm 116)

One: Is there anybody here who loves my Jesus?

Many: I love the Lord.
He heard my voice.
He heard my cry.
He heard my plea.

One: Is there anybody here who loves my Jesus?

Many: I love the Lord
He bent down low to hear me.
He cares for me
And I will trust him as long as I live.

One: Is there anybody here who loves my Jesus?

Many: I love the Lord.
As long as I live I will trust him.
As long as I live I will praise him.
As long as I live I will serve him.

(Kwasi I. Kena, Third Sunday of Easter, Year A)

Renew Us, O God, with Your Spirit

(Psalm 104:24-34)

Many: Renew us, O God, with your Spirit.

One: The earth is full of your creatures.
Pray a short prayer for humankind and the people of God.
End with: Renew us, O God, with your Spirit.

Many: Renew us, O God, with your Spirit.

One: Living things both great and small look to you for provisions.
Pray a short prayer for the earth and all creation.
End with: Renew us, O God, with your Spirit.

Many: Renew us, O God, with your Spirit.

One: Yonder is the sea great and wide.
Pray a short prayer for the witness of the church in the world.
End with: Renew us, O God, with your Spirit.

Many: Renew us, O God, with your Spirit.

One: I will sing to the Lord as long as I live;
I will sing praises to my God while I have being.
Pray a short prayer for the music ministry.
End with: Renew us, O God, with your Spirit.

Many: Renew us, O God, with your Spirit.

One: May our meditations be pleasing to you.
Pray a short prayer for the ministry of Word.
End with: Let us rejoice in the Lord. Renew us, O God, with your Spirit.

All: Renew us, O God, with your Spirit—in the name of Jesus Christ. Amen!

(Marilyn E. Thornton, Day of Pentecost, Year A)

Father Abraham, Mother Sarah

(Genesis 12:1-9)

One: Father Abraham has many sons.

**Many: Black ones and white ones
Yellow, brown, and red ones.**

All: We all claim Father Abraham!

One: Mother Sarah has many daughters.

**Many: Poor ones and rich ones
Young ones, retired ones.**

All: We all claim mother Sarah!

One: I have a story, you have a story, and God has a story.
Look for yourself in the beginning of the story
Of Father Abraham.

Many: And Mother Sarah.

All: And all people of faith!

(Safiyah Fosua, Third Sunday after Pentecost, Year A)

We Will Call on Your Name as Long as We Live
(Psalm 116:1-2; 12-19)

One: When I woke up this morning and saw that God had given me another chance, I made up my mind that I would . . .
Many: Call on the Lord as long as I live.

One: When I realized that God's ear was turned toward me when I cried for mercy for my sin, I decided that I would . . .
Many: Call on the Lord as long as I live.

One: Though death sought to cancel my dreams,
and the grave tried to bury my blessings;
though trouble turned my triumphs into tears,
and sorrow saddened my hopes for tomorrow,
God, you still watched over me,
your protecting hand keeps on holding me,
and for that I'm clear that I will . . .
Many: Call on you as long as I live.

One: How can we repay you, God, for all the goodness you have shown to us?
Many: We will call on your name as long as we live.

One: We will lift up the cup of salvation, telling the marginalized in the streets and the disenfranchised in the home that your grace and mercy endure forever.

Many: We will call on your name as long as we live.

One: We will fulfill our vows to you, God, in the presence of your people, loving you through loving our neighbor.
Many: We will call on your name as long as we live.

One: You've freed us from the chains of Egypt, sustained us across the Atlantic Ocean, and kept us alive from slavery to the present day. We promise to serve you and . . .

Many: We will call on your name as long as we live.

One: As we assemble to worship you today, bringing our offerings and fulfilling our vows to you, Lord God,
All: May we forever call on your name, yes, as long as we live.
We've come to worship the Lord!

(Joseph W. Daniels, Jr., Fourth Sunday after Pentecost, Year A)

Sin Done Lost Its Grip on Me
(Romans 6:12-23)

One: In the passion of the moment, at the point of no return, God's grace took hold of me and continues to keep me whole.
Many: Sin done lost its grip on me.

One: In the greed of this generation and in the selfishness of this society, God's mercy still chases me and rests securely around my soul.
Many: Sin done lost its grip on me.

One: In my failure to love my neighbor, in my failure to love myself, in my desire to love the world before God and anything else, still I'm rescued by a divine love that, in my wretchedness, refuses to let me go. I tell you,
Many: Sin done lost its grip on me.

One: In my rebellion against God, in my devastation and despair, there's a heavenly hand that holds me and cares.
Many: Yes, sin done lost its grip on me.

One: When I want to do right, but end up doing wrong; when the good I want to do, I don't do; and the evil I don't want to do, I do–still I see that God's grace is sufficient because
Many: Sin done lost its grip on me.

One: We've been brought from death to life.
Many: Sin done lost its grip on us.

One: We've been made instruments of God's righteousness.
Many: Sin done lost its grip on us.

One: We've been set free from transgression.
Many: Sin done lost its grip on us.

One: So emerge from your guilt; rise up from your shame. Return to the game. There's something about his name.
Many: Sin done lost its grip on us.

One: Remember that the wages of sin is death, but the gift of God is eternal life in Christ Jesus our Lord. Rejoice, for . . .

All: SIN DONE LOST ITS GRIP ON US!

(Joseph W. Daniels, Jr., Sixth Sunday after Pentecost, Year A)

Lord, Show Us Your Steadfast Love

(Psalm 13)

How long, O Lord, will we be destroyed by drive-bys, ravaged by gentrification, and misinformed through mis-education?
Lord, show us your steadfast love and cause us to rejoice in your salvation.

How long, O Lord, will economic injustice, unemployment and underemployment, domestic violence and depression gain victory over us?
Lord, show us your steadfast love and cause us to rejoice in your salvation.

How long, O God, will marriage mishaps, family fractures, down-low disguises, and the sadness of searching singles cause pain in our souls and sorrow in our hearts all the day long?
Lord, show us your steadfast love and cause us to rejoice in your salvation.

We come this morning looking for an answer from the Lord, who shines light into darkness and brings hope to replace despair. O God, our help in ages past, our hope in years to come, we come now to worship you. For in our singing and praise to you, we know that you will deal bountifully with us. You will hear and answer our prayers! Let us worship God!
Lord, show us your steadfast love and cause us to rejoice in your salvation!

(Joseph W. Daniels, Jr., Sixth Sunday after Pentecost, Year A)

God Meant It for Good!

Somebody meant it for evil, but God meant it for good!

When he summoned famine against the land,
and broke every staff of bread,
he had sent a man ahead of them,
Joseph, who was sold as a slave. *(Psalm 105:16-17)*

Somebody meant it for evil, but God meant it for good!

His feet were hurt with fetters,
his neck was put in a collar of iron;
until what he had said came to pass,
the word of the LORD kept testing him. *(Psalm 105:18-19)*

Somebody meant it for evil, but God meant it for good!

The king sent and released him;
the ruler of the peoples set him free,
He made him lord of his house,
and ruler of all his possessions,
to instruct his officials at his pleasure,
and to teach his elders wisdom *(Psalm 105:20-22)*,
that they might keep his statutes,
and observe his laws,
Praise the LORD! *(Psalm 105:45b)*

(Tony Peterson, Twelfth Sunday after Pentecost, Year A)

Sometimes a Brother Don't Act Like a Brother
(Genesis 37:1-4, 12-28)

One: Joseph was shepherding the flock with his brothers; and Joseph brought a bad report of them to their father. (Genesis 37:2)

Many: Sometimes a brother don't act like a brother, but there is a Friend who sticks closer than a brother.

One: Now Israel loved Joseph more than any other of his children, because he was the son of his old age; and he had made him a long robe with sleeves. But when his brothers saw that their father loved him more than all his brothers, they hated him, and could not speak peaceably to him.

Many: Sometimes a brother don't act like a brother, but there is a Friend who sticks closer than a brother.

One: Now his brothers went to pasture their father's flock near Shechem. And Israel said to Joseph, "Go now, see if it is well with your brothers and with the flock; and bring word back to me." So he sent him from the valley of Hebron. So Joseph went after his brothers, and found them at Dothan.

They saw him from a distance, and before he came near to them, they conspired to kill him. They said to one another, "Here comes this dreamer. Come now, let us kill him and throw him into one of the pits; then we shall say that a wild animal has devoured him, and we shall see what will become of his dreams."

Many: Sometimes a brother ain't much of brother, but there is a Friend who sticks closer than a brother.

One: But when Reuben heard it, he delivered him out of their hands, saying, "Let us not take his life." Reuben said to them, "Shed no blood; throw him into this pit here in the wilderness, but lay no hand on him"–that he might rescue him out of their hand and restore him to his father.

Many: Sometimes a brother don't act like a brother, but there is a Friend who sticks closer than a brother.

One: So when Joseph came to his brothers, they stripped him of his robe, the long robe with sleeves that he wore; and they took him and threw him into a pit. The pit was empty; there was no water in it. Then they sat down to eat.

Many: Sometimes a brother ain't much of brother, but there is a Friend who sticks closer than a brother.

One: Then Judah said to his brothers, "What profit is there if we kill our brother and conceal his blood? Come, let us sell him to the Ishmaelites, and not lay our hands on him, for he is our brother, our own flesh."

Many: Sometimes a brother don't act like a brother, but there is a Friend who sticks closer than a brother.

One: When some Midianite traders passed by, they drew Joseph up, lifting him out of the pit, and sold him to the Ishmaelites for twenty pieces of silver. And they took Joseph to Egypt.

All: Sometimes a brother don't act like a brother, but there is a Friend.

(Tony Peterson, Twelfth Sunday after Pentecost, Year A)

Let My People Go
(Exodus 3:1-15)

Choir: Sing
When Israel was in Egypt's Land,
Let my people go,
Oppressed so hard they could not stand,
Let my people go.

Congregation Sing:
Go down, Moses,
Way down in Egypt's Land.
Tell ol' Pharaoh,
Let my people go.

Leader Speak:
From the bondage of unwarranted suffering,
From bondage to comfort and ease

People Speak:
From bondage to poverty
From bondage to wealth
From bondage to self-ambition
From bondage to mediocrity

Choir Sing:
No more shall they in bondage toil,
Let my people go,
Let them come out with Egypt's spoil,
Let my people go.

Congregation Sing:
Go down, Moses,
Way down in Egypt's Land.
Tell ol' Pharaoh,
Let my people go.

Leader:
From bondage to self-centeredness
From bondage to self-hatred

People:
From bondage to individualism
From bondage to addictions
From bondage to celebrity worship
From bondage to a consumerist culture
From bondage to apathy

Choir Sing:
O let us all from bondage flee,
Let my people go,
And let us all in Christ be free,
Let my people go.

Congregation Sing:
Go down, Moses,
Way down in Egypt's Land.
Tell ol' Pharaoh,
Let my people go.

Leader:
Rise, let us enter the promised land of community

People:
the promised land of sacrifice for others
the promised land of self-control
the promised land of transformation

Choir Sing:
Your foes shall not before you stand,
Let my people go,
And you'll possess fair Canaan's land,
Let my people go.

Congregation Sing:
Go down, Moses,
Way down in Egypt's Land.
Tell ol' Pharaoh,
Let my people go.

Leader:
To the promised land of salvation

People:
To the promised land of the reign of God

Choir Sing:
We need not always weep and mourn,
Let my people go,
And wear these slavery chains forlorn,
Let my people go.

Congregation Sing:
Go down, Moses,
Way down in Egypt's Land.
Tell ol' Pharaoh,
Let my people go.

All Sing:
Go down, Moses,
Way down in Egypt's Land.
Tell ol' Pharaoh,
Let my people go.

(Tony Peterson, Fifteenth Sunday after Pentecost, Year A)

Let's Lift Our Hands and Just Praise

(Psalm 149)

One: Praise the Lord and sing to the Lord a new song.
Many: Let's lift our voices and just praise the Lord!

One: Let the people rejoice in God their maker, and let all the children be filled with joy.
Many: Let's lift our hands and just praise the Lord!

One: Praise the Lord with dancing and singing, timbrels and harps.
Many: Let's lift our souls and just praise the Lord!

One: Let the saints of God be joyful and let them sing aloud all the day long.
Many: Let's lift our songs and just praise the Lord!

One: Let there be high praises to God in our mouths and on our lips.
Many: Let's lift our shouts and just praise the Lord!

One: Praise God for mighty deeds of justice, righteousness, and honor.
All: Let's just praise the Lord!

(Eugene Blair, Sixteenth Sunday after Pentecost, Year A)

Who Is Like You, O God?
(Exodus 15:1-18)

One: I will sing to the Lord, for he has triumphed.
Many: Our enemies have been thrown into the sea; they threaten us no more.

One: The Lord is my strength. The Lord gives me a song to sing.
Many: The Lord has been our God, our strength, our praise for many generations.

One: The Lord is greatly to be feared by those who do evil.
Many: The right hand of the Lord is sure, full of excellence, power and righteousness.

One: You cast your enemies into the sea with breath from your nostrils.
Many: Who is like you, O God, glorious and holy?

One: All people will hear of your glorious power and will give you praise.
Many: The mightiest of all nations will fall down and worship you.

(Eugene Blair, Seventeenth Sunday after Pentecost, Year A)

The First Shall be Last, and the Last Shall be First
(Matthew 20:1-16)

One: Come, let us give an account of our lives to God.
Many: The first shall be last, and the last shall be first.

One: Let us give an account of our stewardship, everything we have done since we said yes to Jesus.
Many: The first shall be last, and the last shall be first.

One: The harvest is great, but there are just a few of us.
Many: The first shall be last, and the last shall be first.

One: We must work while it is day because when night comes, none of us will be able to work.
Many: The first shall be last, and the last shall be first.

Moments of silent reflection

One: Come, give an account of your stewardship, everything you have done since you said yes to Jesus.

Many: The last shall be first, and the first shall be last; for many are called, but few chosen. Amen.

(Eugene Blair Eighteenth Sunday after Pentecost, Year A)

Tell Us a Story

(Psalm 78:1-4, 12-16)

One: Listen up people, open your ears to what I have to say.

Many: Open your mouth and tell us a story just like the parables of old.

One: Well, you want me to tell you what you have heard and known, what the old folks have already told you?

Many: Yes, tell us again.

One: Do not hide the love and the law of the Lord from your children.

Many: We must tell them the praises, power, and might of the Lord.

One: We must tell them of the wonderful strength of the Lord and the great things he has done for us.

Many: Yes, we must tell the children of the marvelous works God did in the sight of the old folks in the old days.

One: He rescued us from slavery; he was a bridge over troubled waters; he led us by day and night.

Many: He gave us water when we were thirsty, food when we were hungry, our shepherd by day and night.

One: Listen up people, open your ears to what I have to say.

All: We must be storytellers and story listeners too! For our children must know the great deeds of the Lord.

(Eugene Blair, Nineteenth Sunday after Pentecost, Year A)

Nobody Told Us

One: Lord, nobody told us that the road would be easy.
Many: But we don't believe you brought us this far to leave us.

One: Lord, nobody told us headaches and heartaches wouldn't come.
Many: But we don't believe you brought us this far to leave us.

One: Lord, nobody told us we wouldn't study long, and sometimes study wrong.
Many: But we don't believe you brought us this far to leave us.

One: Lord, nobody told us we wouldn't mistake your voice for the voice of the Evil One.
Many: But we don't believe you brought us this far to leave us.

One: Lord, nobody told us our kindness would not be taken for weakness.
Many: But we don't believe you brought us this far to leave us.

One: Lord, you told us you'd never leave us, so you sent us Jesus Christ. Through Jesus we experience your presence and your deliverance.

All: And so, Lord, we praise you and thank you for giving us Jesus! He righted our wrongs and showed us how to right them. We knew you didn't bring us this far to leave us. Praise the Lord! Praise Jesus Christ!

Optional, sing "I Don't Feel Noways Tired," #175 Songs of Zion

(Sherrie Dobbs Johnson, Twenty-fourth Sunday after Pentecost, Year A)

Clothe Us

(Luke 24:49)

We strip ourselves of the desire to live
according to our will.

Clothe us in the Holy Spirit.

We strip ourselves of doubts and fears.
Clothe us in the Holy Spirit.

We strip ourselves of the oppression and hatred
that attempt to hold us.
Clothe us in the Holy Spirit.

We strip ourselves of bitterness, frustration,
and anger.
Clothe us in the Holy Spirit.

We strip ourselves of the stubbornness that
keeps us from moving where you have
commanded us to go.

Clothe us in the Holy Spirit.

We strip ourselves of the evil
that calls to us daily.
Clothe us in the Holy Spirit.

We strip ourselves of the complacency that
keeps us from truly being your disciples.
Clothe us in the Holy Spirit.

With all that calls to us, Lord, we are
weakened when we dress
ourselves in the ways of
this world. Our strength
comes from you alone.
**Clothe us with your power,
Lord. Clothe us in the
Holy Spirit.**

(Ciona D. Rouse, General Use)

Healing for the World

O God of all creation you have fearfully and wonderfully fashioned us and breathed Your life into us; from the crown of our heads to the soles of our feet, Lord Reign.
Reign in us, Precious Savior, Reign.

As the Great Physician who healed the woman at the well, you are the same Wonder who finds us in the uttermost parts of the world to heal us mind, spirit, and body
Awesome Healer, rescue and deliver, even now.

As the Master Potter and Crafter who takes broken things and mends them back together again.
Melt us and mold us into the restored children, women, and men that you have destined us to be.
Providing Shepherd who charts the path ahead of us, who both precedes and follows us

Place your hand of blessing on our heads and shepherd our souls
We find refuge and rest in your care.
God of Justice, Lord of Lords who never sleeps or slumbers, awaken your vessels throughout the world to rally for freedom and righteous living of your people.
Let us not rest until your *healing* freedom is made know to the world.
We bless your Holy Name and we praise you for being the God who heals not only our bodies but also our souls.

God is a Wonder. Hallelujah, God reigns!

(Stacey Cole Wilson, General Use)

If It Had Not Been for the Lord

(Psalm 124. For use a suggested of this litany in a worship service, see
Black History Month Celebration *on page 221.)*

One: If the LORD had not been on our side–
Many: Let all the people say, if the LORD had not been on our side

One: If the LORD had not been on our side–let Israel say–
**Many: If the LORD had not been on our side when we were attacked,
when anger flared like a flash fire against us.**

One: If the LORD had not been on our side, our enemies would have swallowed us
alive.
Many: Our ancestors would have all perished in the Middle Passage.

One: Our ancestors would have all died in slavery in the Americas
**Many: If the LORD had not been on our side–let all the people say–if the
Lord** had not been on our side, the flood would have engulfed us.

One: If the LORD had not been with us, the torrent would have swept us into the
seas; the raging waters would have swept us away.
Many: Praise the LORD who has not let us be torn by their teeth.

One: Praise the LORD, we have escaped like a bird out of the fowler's snare.
Many: Praise the LORD, the snare has been broken, and we have escaped.

One: Our help is in the name of the LORD, the maker of heaven and earth.
Many: God is our help, the maker of heaven and earth.

**ALL: Our help is in the name of the LORD, the maker of heaven and
earth.**

(Valerie Bridgeman Davis)

Choral Readings

Oh, Prophet, Don't We Know?

(This reading may be divided into single voices or groups representing each number.)

1: Oh, Isaiah, don't we know? Haven't we heard how you waited for the One who would bring peace forever? You waited for desert lands to become springs of life. You waited, waited.

1 and 2: Waited, waited.

ALL: So steady, so strong.

2: Oh, Jeremiah, don't we know you, too? How you waited for Messiah, our saving grace, to come and reign and build a new promise between God and God's people. Persecuted, you waited, waited.

2 and 3: Waited, waited.

ALL: So steady, so strong.

3: Oh yes, John, we know you. How you waited for true light to come into the world. You prepared the way for the King. You waited, waited.

3 and 1: Waited, waited.

ALL: So steady, so strong.

1: Yes, Mary, don't we know you? You, with the unimagined pregnancy, faced stares and embarrassment as you waited to birth the glory of God, our Savior. For nine months, you waited, waited.

1 and 2: Waited, waited.

ALL: So steady, so strong.

3: We are weary, Lord.

2: Desperate for peace.

1: Longing for eternal joy. And we believe God's promise that

ALL: Jesus will come again.

1: So we wait

1 and 2: Wait!

ALL: Wait!

3: So steady,

1 and 2: So steady,

ALL: So strong.

(Ciona D. Rouse, Third Sunday in Advent, Year A)

Let Us Dance the Sacred Dance of the King

All Leaders: Mary's baby, sweet baby boy, has come! Let us dance the Sacred Dance of the King!

Leader 1: And Mary's baby, sweet Son of God, is born to move us over the gap separating us from God's kingdom when we join in the Sacred Dance of the King!

Leader 2: Rejoice today! Mary's baby, our sweet salvation, arrives with both hands reaching asking us to lift him up and step joyfully in the Sacred Dance of the King!

Leader 3: We wrap Mary's baby, sweet Lamb of God, in our arms and share him with the world as we spin and sway, bounce and prance, step and clap the Sacred Dance of the King!

All Leaders: Behold Mary's Baby! Behold the Son of God! Behold our Savior! Behold the Lamb!

*Suggestions: The three leaders may hold colorful cloths or tiny banners to sway, spin, and move in celebration as they read. Or if you have liturgical dancers in your congregation, they can move** to the litany as the leaders read.

**This is suggested movement. Modify according to liturgical dancer's (or dancers') needs and skills.

Mary's baby, *(3-point turn)*

Sweet baby boy, has come (looking down, cradle imaginary baby in arms and rock)

Let us dance *(lunge right, lead right arm)*
the Sacred Dance *(lunge left, lead left arm)*
of the King! *(on toes, raise arms up and then lower arms down and slightly back in a soft curve, spin)*

And Mary's baby *(3-point turn)*
sweet Son of God, is born *(looking down, cradle imaginary baby in arms and rock)*
to move us over the gap *(two steps and a leap)*
separating us from God's *(lead right arm to side, lead left arm to side)*
kingdom (bring both arms forward, crossing hands)
when we join in the Sacred Dance of the King! *(on toes, raise arms up and then lower arms down and slightly back in a soft curve, spin)*

Rejoice today! *(drop to knees with hands still raised)*

Mary's baby, our sweet salvation, arrives *(looking down, cradle imaginary baby in arms and rock)*
with both hands reaching *(one knee up and leaning forward as arms reach forward)*
asking us to lift him up *(rise from knees)*
and step joyfully *(step right then left with arms following)*
in the Sacred Dance of the King! *(on toes, raise arms up and then lower arms down and slightly back in a soft curve, spin)*

We wrap Mary's baby *(3-point turn)*,
sweet Lamb of God, in our arms *(looking down, cradle imaginary baby in arms and rock)*
and share him with the world *(arms forward and out)*

as we spin and sway *(3-point turn in opposite direction of first turn)*
bounce and prance *(leap)*
step and clap *(step right, clap; step left, clap)*
the Sacred Dance of the King! *(on toes, raise arms up and then lower arms down and slightly back in a soft curve, spin)*

Behold Mary's Baby! *(lunge to the right raise arms)*

Behold the Son of God! *(lunge to the left, raise arms)*

Behold our Savior! *(step forward, raise arms)*

Behold the Lamb! *(bring arms down to side and kneel)*

(Ciona D. Rouse, Christmas Eve or Christmas, Years A, B, C)

The Joy of Forgiveness

(Psalm 3, New Living Translation)

VOICE 1: Oh, what joy for those whose rebellion is forgiven, whose sin is put out of sight! Yes, what joy for those whose record the Lord has cleared of sin, whose lives are lived in complete honesty!

All: When I refused to confess my sin, I was weak and miserable, and I groaned all day long.

VOICE 2: Day and night your hand of discipline was heavy on me. My strength evaporated like water in the summer heat!

All: Finally, I confessed all my sins to you and stopped trying to hide them.

VOICE 3: I said to myself, "I will confess my rebellion to the Lord." And you forgave me! All my guilt is gone.

VOICE 1: Therefore, let all the godly confess their rebellion to you while there is time, that they may not drown in the floodwaters of judgment.

All: For you are my hiding place; you protect me from trouble. You surround me with songs of victory.

VOICE 3: The Lord says, "I will guide you along the best pathway for your life. I will advise you and watch over you. Do not be like a senseless horse or mule that needs a bit and bridle to keep it under control."

VOICE 2: Many sorrows come to the wicked, but unfailing love surrounds those who trust the Lord.

All: So rejoice in the Lord and be glad, all you who obey him! Shout for joy, all you whose hearts are pure!

(Carolyn W. Dandridge and Catrinia N. Harrison, First Sunday in Lent, Year A)

Our Times Are in Your Hands

(Psalm 31:9-16. This reading is part of the Liturgy of the Passion for Palm Sunday. This Choral Reading is also appropriate for use at other Holy Week services. Requires at least six readers.)

Readers 1 and 2: Do you see that? Do you see trouble in the world?
Reader 3: My eyes grow weak from seeing the trouble in the world
Readers 3 and 4: My eyes grow weak with sorry; my soul and my body with grief
Reader 2 and 4: I'm tired of looking at death, disease, destruction
Reader 5: I'm weary of groaning, being consumed with anguish
Readers 1 and 6: Do you see that? Do you see the trouble in the world?

All: Lord, have mercy, crucifixion on the way!

Reader 2: I'm tired of being weak, of my strength failing
Reader 4: I'm tired of being afraid of my neighbors
Reader 5: My bones are weak

All: Do you think Jesus felt this way: weak, tired, weary?

Readers 4, 5, and 6: In the face of distress, people who did not believe?
Readers 1, 2, and 3: In a world full of sorrow?

All: Lord, have mercy, what distress!

Reader 1: Do you think people run from Jesus, too?

All Readers *(Repeated, some on top of other voices)*: **WHAT**

Reader 1: Shattered legacy; world so full of terror on every side . . .
Readers 1 and 2: Do you see that?
Reader 3 and 4: Can you trust in God?
Reader 5: What, and say, "You are my God?"

All: Yes, and say, "You are my God!" How else do you face the uncertainty?

Reader 3: How else do you face the uncertainty? How else?

All *(Repeat several times)*: **Oh, God! Our times are in your hands; our times are in your hands**

Reader 6: Deliver us and let your face shine on your servants

All *(Repeat several times)*: **Are we the servants?**

All: Let your face shine on us! Servants?

Readers 1 and 2: Let your face shine on us servants

All: Save us with your love that never fails

Readers 5 and 6: Never fails! Love! In distress

All: Love! Never failing love!

All *(Repeat several times over voices, each, some together, some staggered)*: **Lord, have mercy: Love!**

(Valerie Bridgeman Davis Palm Sunday, Year A)

It's the Same Spirit
(1 Corinthians 12:3b-13)

Choir *(Sung)*: Every time I feel the Spirit moving in my heart I will pray.
(Songs of Zion, 121. Sing melody in unison, refrain only.)

Group 1: No one can say, "Jesus is Lord"
except by the Holy Spirit.
Now there are varieties of gifts,
but the same Spirit;
and there are varieties of services but the same Lord.

Group 2: There are varieties of activities,
but it is the same God
who activates all of them in everyone.
To each is given
the manifestation
of the Spirit
for the common good.

Choir *(Sung)*: I'm gonna sing when the Spirit says sing *(3 times)* and obey the Spirit of the Lord.
(Songs of Zion, 81. Sing melody in unison.)

Group 1: To one is given through the Spirit the utterance of wisdom, and to another the utterance of knowledge according to the same Spirit.

Choir *(Sung)*: I'm gonna preach when the Spirit says preach *(3 times)* and obey the Spirit of the Lord.
(Songs of Zion, 81. Sing melody in unison.)

Group 2: To another faith by the same Spirit, to another gifts of healing by the one Spirit.

Choir *(Sung)*: I'm gonna pray when the Spirit says pray *(3 times)* and obey the Spirit of the Lord.
(Songs of Zion, 81. Sing melody in unison.)

Group 1: To another the working of miracles, to another prophecy, to another the discernment of spirits.

Group 2: To another various kinds of tongues, to another the interpretation of tongues.

Choir *(Sung)*: I'm gonna shout when the Spirit says shout and obey the Spirit of the Lord.
(Songs of Zion, 81. Sing melody in unison.)

Both Groups: All these are activated by one and the same Spirit, who allots to each one individually just as the Spirit chooses.

Choir *(Sung)*: Every time I feel the Spirit moving in my heart I will pray. Every time I feel the Spirit moving in my heart I will pray.
(Songs of Zion, 121. Sing in harmony.)

(Marilyn E. Thornton, Day of Pentecost, Year A)

Jesus Is a Rock in a Weary Land

(Psalm 46:1-78, NRSV)

Choir *(Refrain only)*:
Jesus is a Rock in a weary land, a weary land, a weary land.
Jesus is a rock in a weary land, a shelter in a time of storm. *(222,* African American Heritage Hymnal*)*

Group 1: God is our refuge and strength, a very present help in trouble.

Group 2: Therefore we will not fear, though the earth should change, though the mountains shake in the heart of the sea.

Group 1: Though its waters roar and foam.

Group 2: Though the mountains tremble with its tumult.

Choir *(Refrain only)*: Jesus is a Rock in a weary land, a weary land, a weary land. Jesus is a rock in a weary land, a shelter in a time of storm. *(222,* African American Heritage Hymnal*)*

Group 1: There is a river whose streams make glad the city of God.

Group 2: God is in the midst of the city! It shall not be moved.

Group 1: The nations are in an uproar, the kingdoms totter;

Group 2: God speaks and the earth melts.

Both Groups: The Lord of hosts is with us; the God of Jacob is our refuge.

Choir *(Refrain only)*: Jesus is a Rock in a weary land, a weary land, a weary land. Jesus is a rock in a weary land, a shelter in a time of storm. (222, *African American Heritage Hymnal*)

(Marilyn E. Thornton, Second Sunday after Pentecost, Year A)

A Dramatic Reading of Scripture: Genesis 45:1-5

(Adapted from Genesis 45:1-15, CEV)

Female Voice: When Joseph was alone with his brothers, he told them,

Male Voice: "I am Joseph."

Female Voice: Then he cried so loudly that the Egyptians heard him and told about it in the king's palace. Joseph asked his brothers if his father was still alive, but they were too frightened to answer. Joseph told them to come closer to him, and when they did, he said:

Male Voice: Yes, I am your brother Joseph, the one you sold into Egypt. Don't worry or blame yourselves for what you did. God is the one who sent me ahead of you to save lives. Now hurry back and tell my father that his son Joseph says, "God has made me ruler of Egypt. Come here as quickly as you can. You will live near me in the region of Goshen with your children and grandchildren, as well as with your sheep, goats, cattle, and everything else you own. I will take care of you there during the next five years of famine. But if you don't come, you and your family and your animals will starve to death."

Female Voice: Joseph and Benjamin hugged each other and started crying. Joseph was still crying as he kissed each of his other brothers. After this, they started talking with Joseph.

(Tony Peterson, Thirteenth Sunday after Pentecost, Year A)

Our Help is in the Name of the LORD

(Psalm 124, NRSV)

All: Our help is in the name of the LORD, who made heaven and earth.

One voice: If it had not been the LORD who was on our side

All: Our help is in the name of the LORD, who made heaven and earth.

Two Voices: If it had not been the LORD who was on our side, when our enemies attacked us,

All: Our help is in the name of the LORD, who made heaven and earth.

Three Voices: If it had not been the LORD who was on our side then they would have swallowed us up alive, when their anger was kindled against us;

All: Our help is in the name of the LORD, who made heaven and earth.

Four Voices: If it had not been the LORD who was on our side then the flood would have swept us away, the torrent would have gone over us;

All: Our help is in the name of the LORD, who made heaven and earth.

Three Voices: If it had not been the LORD who was on our side then over us would have gone the raging waters.

All: Our help is in the name of the LORD, who made heaven and earth.

Two Voices: Blessed be the LORD, who has not given us as prey to their teeth.

All: Our help is in the name of the LORD, who made heaven and earth.

One Voice: We have escaped like a bird from the snare of the fowlers; the snare is broken, and we have escaped.

All: Our help is in the name of the LORD, who made heaven and earth.

Our help is in the name of the LORD, who made heaven and earth!

(Tony Peterson, Fourteenth Sunday after Pentecost, Year A)

Prayers of Confession

Calls to Confession

(Matthew 4:12-23)

Friends, a light has dawned on the earth in Jesus, and still we stumble in the dark. We have been called to repentance for the reign of heaven has come near. Let us confess our rebellion and our resistance to follow the one who calls us and lays claim to our lives.

(Valerie Bridgeman Davis, Third Sunday after Epiphany, Year A)

Friends, God moves among us, sometimes blatantly, sometimes hidden, but we fail to recognize God's movement and fail to live as faithful witnesses of this movement. Come, let us confess our sins before God and one another and be chastised, strengthened, and forgiven.

(Valerie Bridgeman Davis, Ph.D., Second Sunday of Easter, Year A)

(Genesis 32:22-31)

"What is your name?" Jacob's combatant demanded. He may as well have said, "Who are you–really?" A name was often descriptive of personal traits and character in Old Testament culture.

"What is your name?" The question was a call to confession–daring an honest response. Stubborn resistance held Jacob's adversary at bay. Jacob was not losing, but he wanted a blessing.

"What is your name? *"*What should I to do—wrestle all night for nothing or confess and be blessed?

Jacob! My name is Jacob, trickster, deceiver . . . and I need a blessing today.

(Kwasi I. Kena, Eleventh Sunday after Pentecost, Year A)

Prayers of Confession

Almighty God, forgive us. We have sung "O Come All Ye Faithful," while we exclude people who don't look like us from worship. We have sung "Joy to the World," while millions of people are dying of hunger. We have sung "Go, Tell It on the Mountain," without inviting a single person into a loving relationship with you. Empower us with the desire to live out what we say we believe. Help us be mindful of every opportunity to share the Good News with everyone we meet.

(Junius Dotson, Second Sunday in Advent, Year A)

We confess, Lord, that sometimes we approach your throne believing it's our birthright to be called beloved by you. We say our parents built this church, forgetting that the church belongs to you. We wear our status to show we deserve your love, forgetting that Jesus embraced the outcasts. Sometimes we are clothed like the Pharisees, thinking we can be baptized without changing our lives. Forgive us, dear Jesus. Clothe us, instead, like John preparing the way for you to come. Amen.

(Ciona D. Rouse, Second Sunday in Advent, Year A)

Lord, we confess that we are anxious. As we prepare to celebrate the Messiah's birth, we also wait for Jesus to come again. Sometimes we are hopeless when we think of peace. Sometimes we are doubtful when we think of healing. Sometimes we cannot imagine what it will be like to see your full glory. Yes, we wait; but we confess that we are sometimes impatient, Lord.

(Ciona D. Rouse, Third Sunday in Advent, Year A)

Lord we confess that we suffer today because of sin, both the sins we have chosen and the sins committed against us. We have done things we should not have done, and we have neglected to do those things we should have done. Save us from ourselves; save us from the forces of Evil in this world.

We do not have the power to undo what has already been done, so grant us grace to bear present burdens and courage to change things that can be changed.

Teach us how to live as those prepared to die and dwell eternally with you and your Boy Child, our Savior, Jesus Christ.

Silent Confession

(Sherrie Dobbs Johnson, General, Advent, Year A)

It's the Day after Christmas

(Note: This litany of confession will need to be modified to account for date specific language.)

It's the day after Christmas
    And all through the house
    Is there praise for our Savior
    By children or spouse?

Yesterday our home was noisy
    With excitement and glee
    As children and grown folks thought
    Which gifts are for me?

Forgive us Lord

For paying our gifts so much attention
    That we paid your miraculous birth no heed.

Forgive us Lord

For getting impatient with our "religious relative"
    Who insisted that we pause to offer thanks for your birth.

Forgive us Lord

For spending too much on gifts
    That yield temporary happiness.

Forgive us Lord

For amassing so many Christmas memories
    That barely mentioned your name.

Forgive us Lord

Remind us of the miracle of your birth
    The significance of your life

The sacrifice of your death

So that we may live anew as your children.

(Kwasi I. Kena, Day after Christmas, Year A)

We Long for Light
(Isaiah 9:1-4 and Psalm 27)

One: We, your people, have walked in darkness too long.
Many: Today, Lord, we bow before you in search of the light of hope.

One: We, your people, have wandered into darkness too often.
Many: Today, Lord, we ask for clear guidance–light our way.

One: We, your people, have embraced dark delights and shunned holiness.
Many: Today, Lord, we confess the secret sins that we thought were hidden from your Light.

One: We, your people, have allowed darkness to take residence in our lives.
Many: Today, Lord, we cry for forgiveness for opening our hearts to what we knew was wrong.

All: Today, Lord, we, your people, choose the Light of Salvation instead of the darkness of sin.

(Kwasi I. Kena, Third Sunday after Epiphany, Year A)

Confessional Prayer
(Matthew 4:12-23)

God,

In Jesus you shone your light to all of us who sat in darkness. We see you now, and your call to discipleship. We confess that we are not eager to follow. It will demand that we leave profitable jobs, sometimes. It will demand that we leave family members and move to other parts of the world, sometimes. It will demand that we see our life work as the work of becoming like Christ. If you don't help us, God, we will not be able to follow. The pull of our comfort is great. We do not easily embrace the unknown. But we want to follow you; give us the power to do so. Amen.

(Valerie Bridgeman Davis, Third Sunday after Epiphany, Year A)

Confession and Petition

We are dry, Lord, like the pavement on a sweltering summer day. Our lives are heated and the streams of our souls sometimes run dry. We catch our tears, but they cannot ease our thirst. We drip in sweat, but this cannot ease the heat. So we beg for only a few drops of refreshing rain to moisten the dryness in our world.

(Ciona D. Rouse, Third Sunday in Lent, Year A)

Confession and Celebration

O God of miracles and mighty deeds, we acknowledge your healing and comforting presence in our lives. We confess that we have been blinded by materialism and driven by consumerism. Open our eyes to a new way of being. Send your anointing and grant us fresh insight for spiritual breakthroughs. Shine the light of your truth into our relationships and grant us victory over every secret and shame. We thank you in advance for healings and renewals in our lives. In the name of Jesus, we pray. Amen.

(Junius Dotson, Fourth Sunday in Lent, Year A)

Confession and Celebration

Lord of peace and power, thank you for being a God of revivals and restorations. We confess our marriage, dating, and parenting relationships need healing. We acknowledge that these relationships are driven more by self than by your Spirit. Loose us from the demons of low-esteem. Empower us with a vision for new life and new possibilities. Grant us the assurance that you can breathe new life into our hopes and dreams, relationships and communities. In the Name of Jesus, we pray. Amen!

(Junius Dotson, Fifth Sunday in Lent, Year A)

Lord, too often we take the easy option. We hide in shame. We avoid our Christian family. We bury ourselves in work. Still, our sin remains untouched and obvious to you. We come today asking for the courage to run to you instead of away from you when we are in trouble. Hear our prayer, Lord. Bend down low to see our sincerity. Guide us along the path of repentance that leads us to reconciliation.

(Kwasi I. Kena, Third Sunday of Easter, Year A)

Lord, Somebody and Something Set Me Off

One: Lord, before I could get in here, somebody said something to set me off. Help me to hold my peace. Don't let them steal my joy!

Many: Lord, before I could get in here, I said something to somebody that set them off. Help me to hold my peace. Don't let me crush anyone's joy!

One: Now, Lord, help me count to ten, or take deep breaths in and out to get over that "small stuff" that I turned into "big stuff."

All: Yes, Lord, help us count to ten, or take deep breaths in and out to get over "our stuff" so we can focus on our Savior, Jesus Christ, "The blessed Lamb of God, who takes away the sins of the whole world."

(Sherrie Boyens-Dobbs, Fifth Sunday of Easter, Year A)

Prayer of Confession

(Unison)

God, you demand such hard things. How can you expect me to love those who abuse me? I'm not your Son. I've got a little of his grace, but what you're talking about is too much for an ordinary person like me. What are you going to do about me? What are you going to do with me? Lord have mercy on old hardened me.

It's only been through your grace and mercy that I have found you. It was only when I put down my "dukes" and let you in that you showed me the power of what love could do. You sent Jesus into my life; Oh what a Wonderful Savior!

"Must Jesus bear the cross alone and all the world go free? No, there's a cross for everyone, and there's a cross for me." Help me to pick up my cross and walk on by grace. Amen.

(Sherrie Boyens-Dobbs, Fifth Sunday of Easter, Year A)

God, we confess that we rarely recognize the Holy Spirit at work, even when She smacks us in the face. Worse yet, even when we do recognize this work of the Spirit, we don't acknowledge that it is you at work in our lives and in the world.

This week you sent angels to watch over us. We barely uttered our thanks. We hurried on our way. Forgive us our inattentiveness and reluctance to credit you loudly and joyously. Teach us to tell our children and our children's children of your goodness. Teach us to tell our parents of your goodness. Teach us to tell even the supermarket clerk of your goodness!

We long to hear the good news of the resurrecting love of Christ Jesus. Still our hearts long enough for us to hear that you are with us. Amen.

(Sherrie Dobbs Johnson, Seventh Sunday of Easter or Ascension Sunday, Year A)

Confession

(Based on Romans 3:23-25; 1:16, this confession may be split and used on separate occasions.)

One: Dear Lord, even as now we are justified by your grace as a gift, even as there is redemption in Christ Jesus, even as you provided atonement for sin by your blood, even as we are justified by faith in Jesus Christ;

Many: We have all sinned and fallen short of the glory of God.

One: We have failed to love all of God's children, including ourselves. We have failed to accept the beautiful blue-black, chocolate, honey-colored, caramel, beige, café-au-lait, yellow, vanilla, and white colors that you have given to all of your people. We have failed to love our kinky, nappy, crinkly, curly, and straight hair. We have refused to see your Spirit in others, whether through round, slanted, almond-shaped, black, brown, green, or blue eyes.

Many: We have all sinned and fallen short of the glory of God.

One: We have not been obedient in lifting up the brokenhearted. We have looked down on the addict, the alcoholic, the poor, the undereducated, the imprisoned, and the jobless. We have failed to put out our hands in ways that show your love.

Many: We have all sinned and fallen short of the glory of God.

One: We have broken your law. We have been greedy, spending more than we have, taking more than our share, buying what we want and begging for what we need. We do not tithe. We do not save. We waste the earth's resources, even as our brothers and sisters do not have enough.

Many: We have all sinned and fallen short of the glory of God.

One: We have rebelled against your love. We have not used the gifts and talents you have given us to glorify you. We have not cherished the drumbeats of our African forebears, the spirituals of our slave ancestors, the creative genius of our gospel and blues singers, the intelligence of the jazz innovators, the wisdom of our stories and proverbs, the linguistic skills of our poets, rappers, and preachers.

Many: We have all sinned and fallen short of the glory of God.

One: Forgive us, Lord, for we know that you preached a gospel of love. Help us to not be ashamed of the gospel; it is the power of God for salvation to everyone who has faith. By the power of your love, help us to love ourselves.

Many: For we are not ashamed of the Gospel of Jesus Christ.

One: Help us to love our neighbor.

Many: For we are not ashamed of the Gospel of Jesus Christ.

One: Help us to love you.

Many: For we are not ashamed of the Gospel of Jesus Christ. Amen.

(Silence)

(Marilyn E. Thornton, Second Sunday after Pentecost, Year A)

Confessional Prayer
(Genesis 18:1-15)

"Our Lord and our God, in the name of Jesus,
we come, today, confessing our sin before you.
It is what it is.

**You see it (sin) for what it is.
Forgive us this day we pray.**

Like Sarah, God, we've doubted you, disbelieving that all things are possible with you.
It is what it is, God.

**You see it (sin) for what it is.
Forgive us this day we pray.**

Like Sarah, God, we've laughed at you,
thinking that your miracles have little chance of lifting our hopes.
It is what it is, God.

**You see it (sin) for what it is.
Forgive us this day, we pray.**

Like Sarah, God, we've lied to you, O God.
Lied to you, lied to our loved ones, lied to co-workers, church members and strangers.
Yes, we've denied truth, even while we are standing face to face with your truth.
It is what it is, God.

You see it (sin) for what it is.

Forgive us this day, we pray.

And help us to know day after day that nothing is too hard for you, Lord.
Fixing our broken relationships is not too hard.
Finding a good paying job is not too hard.
Filling an empty heart is not too hard, God.
All things are possible for you.
And, we thank you that at this appointed time you forgive us.
It is what it is, but it doesn't have to stay that way.

Thank you for making a way out of no way.
In Jesus name we pray. Amen."

(Joseph W. Daniels, Jr., Fourth Sunday after Pentecost, Year A)

Corporate Confessional Prayer
(Genesis 21:8-21)

God, we gather ourselves before you this morning as the family of faith,
in need of your grace in rebuilding and repairing our broken families.

Lord, we confess:
That we have contributed to family dissension and division,
family despair and disappointment . . .
(Silence)

That, we have fathered and mothered children
by women and men other than our own spouses . . .
(Silence)

That, we have allowed jealousy to destroy and disintegrate relationships .
. .
(Silence)

That, we have dismissed family members,
intending to never see them or speak to them again . . .
(Silence)

Lord, we have banished family members to unknown places . . .
where their cries could only be heard by you . . .
(Silence)

Forgive us, God, we pray.

Use us today to be agents of reconciliation.
Use us today to provide for loved ones when and where we can.
Grant us the faith to know that where we have failed,
 you are more than able to make things right.

Please, O God, bless the family members we have banished,
 and move in our hearts so that me may love them unconditionally,
 as you so generously and unconditionally love us.

In the name of Jesus, the Christ, who makes this all quite possible, Amen.

(Joseph W. Daniels, Jr., Fifth Sunday after Pentecost, Year A)

Prayer of Confession

(Romans 7:15-25)

Lord, we come before you this day confessing that we don't understand our own actions. The very things we want to do, we don't do. Too often, we find ourselves doing the very things we hate. We need you this day, Lord.

The bottle we tried to put down,
 we keep picking back up, and our soul is hurting.
The drugs we denied once, again seek to destroy us.
 We need you this day, Lord.
The man or woman we have needed to leave alone,
 but just can't let go, has hurt us again. We need you, Lord.
The chance we had to fix that broken relationship came,
 but anger and rage rose up again,
 inflicting harm and abuse upon the very people we said we loved.
 We need you this day, Lord.
The opportunities we have been praying for came,
 but fear, lack of confidence, and low self-esteem, drove them away.

Lord, the good we want to do, we don't do; and the evil we hate doing, we just keep doing. Lord, what messed up souls we are. We need you now, Lord, this day. Rescue us from works that lead to death; save us from self-destructive behaviors. We submit our lives into your hands right now. Amen.

(Silence)

(Joseph W. Daniels, Jr., Seventh Sunday after Pentecost, Year A)

Call to Confession
A Prayer for Esau

(Genesis 25:29-34)

How often, with regret,
  I reflect on what could have been, Lord.
  If only I had known what you had predestined for me before I
    gave it away,
    ignored its potential,
    and misjudged its value
    to enjoy temporary satisfaction.

First anger, then rage consumed me.
Jealousy poisoned my blood. I ache over my losses.
I have spent too many sleepless nights mulling over missed opportunity.
  Forgive me God
    for being shortsighted
    for despising the gifts that you tried to give me.

Let today mark a new beginning.
Give me strength to bless those who have benefited from what I squandered.
Turn my focus away from the pain of regret to the promise of hope. Amen.

(Kwasi I. Kena, Eighth Sunday after Pentecost, Year A)

Call to Confession

(Psalm 139:1-12; 2-24)

I stand before God knowing that "confession is good for the soul." But the thought of opening up before you is overwhelming. At times, I cannot bear to remember how often I have gone astray. At other times, I cloud my memory, justifying what I know is wrong in your sight. I cannot trust myself to confess my sins as often as I should. I need you to help me to be honest. So, like the psalmist, I say, "Search me Lord." You know me. You know my thoughts. You know where I have been and where I am going. Search me Lord; and if there is any wicked way in me, deliver me and lead me into righteousness.

(Kwasi I. Kena, Ninth Sunday after Pentecost, Year A)

Prayer of Confession

(Unison)

Lord, without saying a word, you know who I am. But you ask me to speak, to honestly confess who I am. I confess that some days I deny the genius that you have placed within me. I settle for mediocrity and avoid the responsibilities of greatness. I confess that other days I ignore Christ within me and practice ungodliness. I confess that I have answered to names that were out of character for Christians. Today I confess that I am who you made me to be: holy, righteous, just, loving, and kind.

(Kwasi I. Kena, Eleventh Sunday after Pentecost, Year A)

Confession

(Romans 12:9-21)

Precious Lord, strip away the mask I wear during the week to "get by". Lay my soul bear before you today. Let me see genuine love. Show me the love that hates evil and holds onto to what is good. Strip away the mask that holds my emotions in check when I should share your love with someone. Let me see the joy of giving to others. Show me the power of blessing those who persecute me. Strip away the mask that grins and lies and let's the world think otherwise about a child of God.

(Kwasi I. Kena, Thirteenth Sunday after Pentecost, Year A)

Prayer of Confession

Sing: "Standin' in the Need of Prayer", 110, *Songs of Zion.*

Like Zacchaeus up in the sycamore tree, we seek a closer walk with you. You have called us, O Lord, to come down from our hiding places: the places of our misdeeds and sin, confusion and misunderstanding, anger and despair. Welcome us into the comfort and love of your open arms. Hear us today as we pray for those whom we have wronged, the things we have left undone, and relationships in turmoil. Walk under our tree and call us down to new life and refreshing grace. Call us down to freedom from sin and release us to live in joy. Amen.

(Eugene Blair, Sixteenth Sunday after Pentecost, Year A)

Prayer of Confession

Lord, you have told us what to do. But this love thing is hard. You've invited us to love you with everything we have; instead we have fallen in love with our jobs, houses, and electronic toys. Loving you intimately is scary and we often opt for another way. You've invited us to live in loving relationship with everyone we encounter, but there are folk who are downright hard to love. We confess our inability to love as we should. We need your forgiveness and help living out this love thing. Free us to love as you do. Amen.

(Lillian C. Smith, Twenty-third Sunday after Pentecost, Year A)

A Prayer of Confession

(Written shortly after the death of U.S. Civil Rights Movement leader Rosa Parks on October 24, 2005.)

The apostle Paul encouraged the Roman Christians to present themselves before God as living sacrifices.

Almighty God, today we confess that we have not been so willing to sacrifice.

> We have preferred comfort, convenience and safety over the need
>   to stand up for what we believe
>   or to sit down and to refuse to move until justice comes.
> We confess that we have been all too willing to let others do what all of us should do.
> We confess fear for physical safety.

We thank you, O God, for the example of Rosa Parks,

> born a woman,
> born a black woman,
> born a black woman in the old South,
>   where it was once both acceptable and legal
>   to discriminate against blacks and women.

We thank you for her example of courage and faith, and pray that when opportunity presents itself we might respond with similar courage and similar faith. Amen.

Who Knows?

Who knows what signal,

what internal sentry,
>   prodded Rosa to sit when the bus driver said: "Get up and move."

Was it her aching feet as some have said?

Was it her pounding head that could not wrap itself around the concept of such inequality?

Or, was it her aching heart, bruised from years of injury compounded with interest?

Perhaps, it was just impossible for her to walk any longer with the spiny pebble of injustice in her shoe, in her life, in her spirit.

Only God knows the signal,

>   the sentry,
>   the prod required for each of us.

Oh God, let there be enough feeling left in me to feel your nudging when it comes.

(Safiyah Fosua, Year A)

Gracious God,

Though we live in a culture that is reluctant to admit guilt, assume responsibility, or ask for forgiveness we are so bold as to pray the words of the psalmist who said:

Search me, O God, and know my heart; test me and know my thoughts. See if there is any wicked way in me, and lead me in the way everlasting (Psalms 139:23-24 NRSV).

Search us, O God, and reveal anything in our lives that stands between us and your love.

Search us, O God, show us our sins so that we might confess them,

Search us, O God, show us places where we have neglected Christian responsibility and then teach us how to live on this earth with each other,

Search us, O God, show us the faces of those we have wronged so that we might seek their forgiveness.

(Silence)

Words of Assurance: We have not been called to this hour of worship to wallow in sin and self-pity. God has promised to forgive our sins when we confess them and to cleanse us from all manner of unrighteousness (1 John 1:9). Rise from your knees as children of God, forgiven from sin and empowered to lead holy lives.

All: AMEN, thanks be to God!

(Safiyah Fosua, Year A)

Words of Assurance

The Word of God is ancient, written long before any of us breathed: written before my father's breath, and his mother's breath, and her father's breath, and his mother's breath. And even still, the Holy Spirit breathes life into it for us today. Praise God! (Romans 15:4)

(Ciona D. Rouse, Second Sunday in Advent, Year A)

Christ is coming again. Believe! God will help our unbelief.

(Ciona D. Rouse, Third Sunday in Advent, Year A)

The One who came as a humble baby,
    Reigns as King of the world.

The One who made earthly kings tremble;
    Brought us great joy.

The One who came to judge humanity's sin,
    Wiped our slate clean with his blood.

Jesus will come again with strength and almighty power,
    Yet he will bring peace and calm.

Let us shout for joy whenever we recognize that Jesus is in our midst. Amen!

(Ciona D. Rouse, Fourth Sunday in Advent, Year A)

Jesus has, indeed, come to save us and show us the way to experience God's love. Jesus will strengthen us to the end, so we may be blameless on the day of our Lord Jesus Christ. (See 1 Corinthians 1:4-8.) Hear the good news: you are forgiven!

(Sherrie Dobbs Johnson, General, Advent, Year A)

Only a loving God would send a Savior to suffer for a sinful and forgetful people. Only a concerned God would put on human flesh and experience the same temptations that we face. Lord Jesus Christ you alone understand our frailties and offer us compassionate help when we are tempted. Thank you for being our merciful and faithful high priest. Thank you for welcoming us into your holy family. Thank you for declaring our names in the presence of your holy congregation. Today we walk assured that you love us, forgive us, and trust us with the precious good news of the gospel. (Hebrews 2:10-18.)

(Kwasi I. Kena, The First Sunday after Christmas, Year A)

Darkness of soul and thought are not permanent. "The people who sat in darkness have seen a great light and for those who sat in the region and shadow of death light has dawned" (Matthew 4:16). Receive God's forgiveness. Walk today as children of the Light.

(Kwasi I. Kena, Third Sunday after Epiphany, Year A)

It is almost impossible to comprehend how much God loves the world! We were broken, "running around with no clue how to live," and God sent Jesus! Jesus did not come to punish us but to show us that we can start again. Though it is hard to believe, believe this truth: in the name of Jesus Christ, you are forgiven!

(Ciona D. Rouse, Second Sunday in Lent, Year A)

God's promise is greater than rain or streams. God promises a Savior sent to redeem and fill us with water eternally. Walking in the will of God, we walk without thirst anymore. Amen.

(Ciona D. Rouse, Third Sunday in Lent, Year A)

Sisters and brothers believe the good news: God did not abandon Christ to the grave and will not abandon us to our many and several deaths. We are participants in Jesus' death and in his resurrection. In Christ, we are raised to life and are witnesses of God's miraculous power. We are forgiven and sworn in to give testimony. Amen.

(Valerie Bridgeman Davis, Second Sunday of Easter, Year A)

The Lord is faithful to hear and forgive. Repent and receive the forgiveness of the Lord. Walk now in the confidence that God hears and forgives, loves and restores.

Walk as one forgiven and tell others of the love of God.

Kwasi I. Kena, Third Sunday of Easter, Year A)

Blessed is the Lamb of God, who takes away the sins of the world. Blessed are we because the Lamb of God has taken away our sins.

(Sherrie Boyens-Dobbs, Fifth Sunday of Easter, Year A)

Jesus said, "If we confess our sins, God is faithful and just, and will forgive our sins and cleanse us from all unrighteousness" (1 John 1:9).

(Sherrie Dobbs Johnson, Seventh Sunday of Easter or Ascension Sunday, Year A)

Friends, hear the good news: God has promised to forgive us and to cleanse us from all unrighteousness if we but confess our sins. In the name of Jesus Christ, you are forgiven.

In the name of Jesus Christ you are forgiven. Glory to God! Glory to God! Amen. (Based on John 1:9.)

(Marilyn E. Thornton, Second Sunday after Pentecost, Year A)

Just as you are no longer a slave in society, you are no longer a slave to sin.
Just as your ancestors were emancipated years ago, you've been freed to live with Christ.
You are dead to sin and alive in Christ. So be free indeed. (Based on Romans 6:1b-11.)

(Joseph W. Daniels, Jr., Fifth Sunday after Pentecost, Year A)

Unison: Thank you, God, for your Son Jesus who will make it all right. Thank you for your Son Jesus. He will heal our sin-sick souls. Thank you, God, for Jesus Christ, our Lord. When we find it difficult to do the right thing, we will place our trust in you. We are convinced that we can do all things through Christ who gives us strength (Philippians 4:13). Glory to God! Amen.

(Joseph W. Daniels, Jr., Seventh Sunday after Pentecost, Year A)

God hears the painful cry of regret that leads to repentance.
Know that the Lord is faithful to forgive and provide grace for new beginnings.
Today, you are forgiven.
Today, rediscover the divine destiny that God has for your life.

(Kwasi I. Kena, Eighth Sunday after Pentecost, Year A)

Hear these words of assurance. The Lord is slow to anger and quick to forgive.
The cleansing power of the Holy Spirit is here today. Receive God's forgiveness
and the Holy Spirit's cleansing. Walk now in the newness of life afforded children
of God.

(Kwasi I. Kena, Ninth Sunday after Pentecost, Year A)

The same God who demands honest confession provides thorough forgiveness.
Receive God's forgiveness today. Live as an authentic Christian: holy, righteous,
just, loving, and kind.

(Kwasi I. Kena, Eleventh Sunday after Pentecost, Year A)

An altar, a pew, a seat on the bus, a kitchen table: all become holy places when we
confess before God. Today, in this holy place, God meets us, hears us and forgives
us. In this holy place, God empowers us with genuine love to share with a hurting
world. Be for God, a holy loving people.

(Kwasi I. Kena, Thirteenth Sunday after Pentecost, Year A)

One: Hear the good news! The tomb is empty! Jesus is risen and goes before us!
The Spirit has come! Go forth and live as people of the Resurrection!

Many: We believe it to be so! Amen.

(Eugene Blair, Sixteenth Sunday after Pentecost, Year A)

Grief, Loss, Lament

Leah's Lament
(Genesis 29:15-28)

Why me Lord?

Is "second choice" the best I can hope for? Where does a second-class person go to escape disdain?

Who gave others the right to make me an imposition? Though married to me, my spouse looks more lovingly toward another.

First consideration—will I ever experience it? My diet is confined to leftovers from the party that I cooked for?

Carnivorous rage consumes me. How can I stop my jealous gaze toward Rachel—the sister I once loved?

Will my destiny lie in the hands of others forever? What of my choice? What of my hopes? What of my dreams?

Why me Lord? Only you can deliver me.

(Kwasi I. Kena, Year A)

For Those Who Have Been Hurt
by Someone They Love
(Psalm 23)

Broken, crushed, angry, confused–how could someone I have known for so long not really know me? Is there anything I could have done that would justify what they've done to me? No, nothing! Should I be shouted out, pushed, mishandled, verbally abused? No, never! Could they have forgotten it's me–that I love them, that I would never intentionally harm my beloved? How do I heal? Who do I turn to?

God whispers, "*I am Your Shepherd, let me provide for you.*"

Where shall I go to escape this pain, you wonder? Where can my mind rest? I keep replaying the pain, the words, the actions over and over again. I wish that there was something or someone on earth that could take my problems away instantly. I hoped to hear, "I'm sorry" or "I forgive you." But, these words don't seem possible. My heart aches and my appetite has become small.

God whispers, "*Let me lead you beside still waters and restore your soul; Let me renew your strength.*"

Umm, thank you, Lord. I ponder the pain and want to just get over it and move on. But, I love this person and am still baffled by their obstinate response, by their hard attitude. God, help me, I cry!

God whispers, "*I stand beside you comforting, protecting, and anointing you with the courage to go forth.*"

Surely, God, I need some goodness right now, with evil all around me. I need to feel some mercy–help, me feel your mercy.

God whispers, "*Surely, my goodness and mercy is pursuing you, meeting you where you need it. Look for it.*"

So, where shall I find peace Lord? Is there a place where my heart can heal?

God whispers, "*Come and dwell in my house, in my heart, forever and ever.*"

(Stacey Cole Wilson, General Use)

Prayer for a Wounded Church

(Written several days after Judicial Decision 1032)

You make life lovely, Lord.
Autumn leaves prove your artistic genius.
Glorious mountains testify as your lasting structures.

Strangers feeding strangers
Proclaim your merciful love.
Where you create, Lord,
You make life so lovely.

In this time of brokenness in our church,
Lord, please do your work.
Intercede where we may be wrong.
Increase where we may be in your will.

Take our church and make it lovely, Lord.
Bring spring where limbs are barren.
Make butterflies where caterpillars crawl.
Show hope where there are tears.
Make us lovely, Lord!

In Jesus' name, Amen.

(Ciona D. Rouse)

Lead Us to the Rock

(Prayer for Those Grieving the Loss of a Loved One)

When our hearts are overwhelmed, God
Lead us to the Rock that is Higher–
Higher than our circumstances,
Higher than our grief,
Strong enough to bear our heavy burdens,
Small enough to be touched and held in our moment of great need

God, we assemble here in your presence
To declare that even in the midst of our great sorrow,
You are comforting us, loving us,
Holding us through this difficult time
You are here speaking to us
Your Word of hope that assures us a day is coming
When death shall be no more
As we gather to honor _____
And to celebrate (his/her) legacy that lives in our hearts
We pause to give you thanks.
Thank you for enabling us to experience (her/his) love.
Thank you for allowing us to know this precious soul fashioned by you.
Thank you for allowing us to further know more of your great love for us
Through _____'s life.

Pour out your Spirit, even now.
Minister to your people in this hour.
In every hand and heart, reign God.
Let your healing waters flow; let your mercy abound here.
Take our tears and multiply our joy.
Take our silence, and magnify your Word in us.
We find rest in you, hope in you, and a reason to live in you.
In the Name of the Father, the Son, and the Holy Spirit, one God Perfect in every
way, we pray. Amen.

(Stacey Cole Wilson, General Use)

Hope in God's Presence

(Psalm 139)

One: *Where* shall we go from your Spirit? In Africa, the Americas, Antarctica, Asia, Australia, Europe, and every place in between, you are there.

Many: Lord, You have not abandoned us.

One: Where shall we escape your presence?

Many: There is not a place where your hand cannot touch and transform us.

One: If we dwell in the uttermost places of life

Many: You are there bringing hope in the midst of despair; joy to those with broken hearts; healing to pains that endeavor to destroy us.

One: Where can we go from your Spirit?

Many: There is not one place we can go.

One: God of grace and mercy, pour out your Spirit upon us and stir up the gifts within us to do tour work in the world. Cause us to be agents of your righteousness, justice, deliverance, and salvation. Continue to work your miracles in us, in our homes, in our relationships, in our finances, in our communities, in this nation, in your world. You are here and there is hope in your presence! So, we rest in you knowing that You are the God who is omnipresent and ever watching over your people. God is here

Many: Saving, healing and delivering us! Hallelujah! We find hope in you, Great Wonder. God is here!

(Stacey Cole Wilson)

Counting Sparrows

On the morning after Christmas 2004, the strongest earthquake seen in forty years triggered huge waves, tsunamis, which engulfed islands, and drowned untold thousands.

What prayer can we say at such a time,
When thousands upon thousands,
Ten thousands upon ten thousands
Are missing – bodies never to be retrieved?

What prayer would make a difference
To those who remain?

So often we have been taught to pray to change things,
to make a difference to stop a tragedy.
But when the tragedy has already come; how do we pray?
Perhaps, 'conventional wisdom' about prayer
must be laid aside on this day.

Hear the words of Jesus, who said:

> Are not two sparrows sold for a penny? Yet not one
> of them will fall to the ground apart from your Father.
> And even the hairs of your head are all counted. So
> do not be afraid; you are of more value than many
> sparrows (Matthew 10:29-31 NRSV).

In the aftermath of one of the most terrible tragedies that any of us can remember, we are comforted by the knowledge that the same God, who knows when a sparrow falls to the ground, knew and loved each of those who died.

On this day, the prayer is one of remembrance:
We remember that those who perished in the tsunamis are
More than numbers,
More than statistics,
More valuable than sparrows;
Each was a person of sacred worth created in the image of God.

Unison Prayer:

Loving God,

We pause to remember the untold thousands of individuals who perished this week. They were people who belonged to cities and villages, commu-

nities and places of worship. With their friends and families we pause to remember that you gave them life and loved them. In our present helpless state, we are comforted to know that you know each person by name. Lord, have mercy upon this earth and all who mourn on this day. Amen.

(Safiyah Fosua)

Lord, Shorten the Distance

(In the wake of the subway bombing in London, July 7, 2005)

A Prayer for Compassion

Lord, shorten the distance
> The tragedy in London seems so distant,
> almost beyond our sense of feeling
> and compassion.

Lord, shorten the distance between my heart and another's calamity.
> Remind me that I truly am part of a global village dear to God.
> Compel me to groan with all of creation awaiting God's ultimate redemption and restoration.

Move me from satisfied spectator
> drowsy from the complacent presumption
> that God will ultimately right all wrongs
> and restore all that has been corrupted.

Move me to avid participator in God's great plan of redemption.
> What can I do to help?
> How can I serve?
> Whom shall I comfort?

Lord, shorten the distance between passivity and fervent intercession.
> Remind me that the prayer of the righteous is powerful and effective.
> Remind me that the world prayed for us on 9/11,
> Now we can reciprocate.

When lethargy toward "those suffering over there" threatens my willingness to be compassionate . . .

Lord, shorten the distance.

(Kwasi I. Kena)

Disaster Meets Prayer Again

(In the wake of Hurricane Katrina in the U.S.)

Disaster and prayer met again
    Shouting and moaning the name *Katrina*

Aching over loss
    Frayed souls huddle close
    Clutching in the darkness for scraps of hope

Frantic desperation
    Groans too deep for words beat against howling winds

Wet with fear
    One survivor mops another's worried brow

Devastated lives
    Redefine "normal" amid chaos and rubble

Raw, intense prayers
    Pour from strained lives

(Kwasi I. Kena, August 30, 2005)

In Search of a Straw

(In the wake of hurricanes Katrina and Rita in the U.S. 2005)

It began as an echo
a hint
whispering: "I might hurt–but then again, maybe not . . ."

Hour upon hour
hinting and flirting
until it emerged
as pain.

Fleeting pain
nagging pain
aching pain
a pain that gnawed and chewed
a pain that signaled and threatened
a pain that made me want to climb the walls
and claw at the windows.

And then, I heard the dreaded 'snap.'
Snapped so hard that it
snapped my mind
snapped my will
snapping in every waking thought
snapping that refused to let me sleep–forget about dream!

Didn't everybody hear the snap
that sounded like thunder on the inside?

Surely if they heard the thunderous sound that snapped inside of me, they would
come and wake me from this eyes-open bad dream.

Perhaps no one will believe how awful it really is
until I crawl through the rubble
and locate the very straw
that broke my back.

(Safiyah Fosua, September 1, 2005)

A Choral Reading of Confession and Confrontation

(Ezekiel 37:1-7 and Psalm 11)

For the devastation and destruction by Hurricane Katrina and ensuing flooding and governmental breakdown

Instructions: There will be people from each group scattered throughout the sanctuary; underlined portions should be read by all the groups.

Group 1: There is a city full of wet bones; bones in the streets and bones in houses; bodies in dress and bodies naked; there is a country full of wet bones

Group 2: O human, Can these bones live, God ask? O, human. Can my people rise from the waters and live again?

Group 3: You know and you alone, Lord. You know, and you alone.

Group 2: There is a city full of wet bones; bodies ravaged by wind and rain; bodies mutilated by rats and alligators; bodies destroyed by nature and human neglect.

There is a city full of wet bones

Group 1: O human, Can these bones live, God asks? O, human, can my people rise from the waters and live again?

Group 3: You know and you alone, Lord. You know, and you alone.

Group 2: NO!!! Says God; YOU prophesy to these bones; YOU speak life to them; YOU confront their death; YOU know, too, whether they will live again; because YOU will be life OR death to them

Group 3: Prophesy to the bones and to the wind; prophesy to the poor and to the powers that be.

Group 2: Prophesy to the bones and to the wind; prophesy to the children and to the corporate moguls.

Group 1: Prophesy to the bones and to the wind; prophesy to the elderly and to the economic benefitters.

Group 1: YES!!! YOU prophesy to these bones; YOU speak life to them; confront their death. You know, too, whether they will live again; because YOU will be life OR death to them.

Group 2: But the foundations are being destroyed, O God; <u>the very fabric of society has been ripped and exposed.</u>

Group 1: We see the disparity of health care; <u>we see the disillusionment of the poor</u>; we see the vulnerability of the aged; we see the abandoned pets.

Group 3: We see the slow response of FEMA; <u>we see the posturing of politicians</u>; we see the overwhelmingly black and brown faces.

<u>Foundations are being destroyed, O God; the very fabric of society ripped and exposed.</u>

Group 2: <u>We see the kindness of strangers</u>; we see the gentleness of young black men caring for children and elders; we see the graciousness of police officers rescuing people from attics.

<u>And the foundations are being destroyed; WHAT CAN WE DO, O GOD?</u>

Group 1: Prophesy to the bones and the wind, O human; <u>tell the truth</u> about what you see.

Group 3: <u>Live in simplicity</u> and share with the less fortunate; take only what you need and <u>share what you have.</u>

Group 2: Insist on justice and care for the most vulnerable among us; <u>tell the truth</u> about what you see.

<u>So, I prophesied as I was commanded. And as I was prophesying, there was a noise, a rattling sound, and the bones came together</u>

<u>Prophesy as commanded</u>

Group 1:<u> We must tell the stories</u> of bodies in the streets.

Group 3:<u> We must tell the stories</u> of a slow-response government.

Group 1:<u> We must tell the stories</u> of poor people–black, white, brown–who could not or would not leave.

Group 2:<u> We must record the horror</u> in the words of the survivors, not in the words of cultural controllers.

<u>We must not let these stories get lost.</u>

<u>We must not let these stories get lost.</u>

(Valerie Bridgeman Davis)

Waiting for (Hurricane) Rita—A Prayer

*(A prayer for those waiting in the path of Hurricane Rita and
for those in other places who join them in prayer)*

Like a tivo-slow-motion-replay of a terrible accident
   is the mention of the name Rita
   layering dread upon souls
   already drenched with misery
   while children with night terrors
   of the rain
   hold tightly to borrowed skirt-tails
   or leap into borrowed arms to
   wail the wail of the dejected.

Have mercy, O God,
   upon your people, we are battered and broken.

Have mercy, O God,
   upon your people, we are weary and worn.

Have mercy, O God,
   upon the world that you created,
   and upon the people who struggle to give you praise in the midst of the
   storm.

Have mercy, O God,
   and grant us peace.

(Safiyah Fosua)

Lord, in Your Mercy Hear Our Prayers

(In the wake of Hurricane Rita, hot on the heels of Hurricane Katrina, in the U.S.)

Lord hear our prayers:

For those stalled in cars and those huddled in homes
For those who are fleeing the storm for
the second time
And for those whose lives are in danger . . .

Lord, in your mercy, hear our prayers . . .

Lord hear our prayers:
For local, state and federal government officials
who were never trained for such severe circumstances

For all who labor and for all who own businesses small and large
For homeowners and renters and for those who live under bridges . . .

Lord, in your mercy, hear our prayers . . .

Lord hear our prayers:
For babies and nursing mothers
For toddlers and old folks
For adolescents and mid-aged people who understand the danger and fear

Lord, in your mercy, hear our prayers . . .

Lord, hear our prayers:
For all creatures great and small
For dogs on the lap and wolves in the wild
For creeping things and things that hop or fly . . .

Lord, in your mercy, hear our prayers . . .

Lord, have mercy upon your people and your creation and your land
In this hour of trial.

(September 23, 2005, Safiyah Fosua)

Why Meets What

(A congregational call to prayer)

Why another storm?
> Why more devastation?

Why more human suffering?
> Our whys go unanswered until we determine what we will do in the mean-time . . .

Prayer moves us toward
> A compassionate "what"
> That lends our hearts
> And hands to God
> When tragedy strikes

Pray with groans
> Pray in silence
> Pray with actions–but by all means pray!

Let us pray for:

> Those who are displaced by the storm–people who continue to live in shelters and with friends;

> The families of those who perished in the storm;

> The many volunteers who fill in for National Guard members who are away at war;

> City, state and national leaders who must find ways to help communities rebuild;

> That we who dwell in safety might open our hearts and our treasure to those who are in need;

(Kwasi I. Kena and Safiyah Fosua)

When the Wind Blows

(While this call was issued in the face of the 2005 hurricane and subsequent floods in southern United States, it might be used in the face of any natural and catastrophic event.)

When the wind blows
When willows bow and snap under the weight of the wind
When the words "catastrophic event" cease to get the same billing as
big screen entertainment
When the words "catastrophic event" cleave instead to our stomach pits
When congregations of raindrops become inland streams flowing where they will
When the streets are littered with wet teddy bears, broken dishes and shattered
dreams
When the wind blows both the wheat and the chaff of our lives in giant swirls
Good Lord, anchor us in your love.

(Safiyah Fosua)

Lament for War

Voice of the Children (led by one or several children):

We have no place to play
No safe water to drink
And our parents are dying
We are being taught hate
We live in fear
Who knows what tomorrow will bring
Or whether you will forget us, if we are not on your evening news

The People's Response:
God, help us!

Voice of the men (led by one or several men):
We do not want to kill
We refuse to go on a death mission
We are sons and brothers of the Prince of Peace
It may get us killed to resist the killing
But we refuse to believe that violence is the only way
We are sons of the Christ who refused the sword
The Christ who reattached the ear
We want to reattach the ears that cannot hear

The People's Response
God, help us!

Voice of the Women (led by one or several women)
Like Rachel crying for her children, we are weeping
We are weeping for our sons, brothers, and fathers
We are weeping for our daughters, sisters, and mothers
Like Rizpah standing for her sons, we are demanding justice and peace
Like Mary we are pondering what will become of this world

The People's Response
God, help us!

(Valerie Bridgeman Davis)

Call to Deliverance from the Lust for War

You have seen with your eyes what our hands have done
[There is a painting on the wall written in red; the scream of mother earth;
the lament of the land]
Our silence will not save us, Audré Lorde said, but we stand silent in the presence
of horrific destruction and loss of life
We are numb to the pain, afraid we will feel ourselves into crying and we will not
stop screaming

The Gathered Response:
God, deliver us!

We are afraid that protest against violence will label us as unpatriotic and anti-
troops
We are afraid that standing with the Prince of Peace will get us killed
We want to be delivered from our silence
We want to be delivered from our complacency

The Gathered Response:
God, deliver us!

We want to be delivered from our complicity when we choose the nation over the
Kingdom of God
We want to be delivered from idolatry
We want to be delivered
We want to be delivered
We want to be delivered

The Gathered Response:
God, deliver us!

(Valerie Bridgeman Davis)

A Prayer of Repentance

One: forgive us, but do not let us forget

The People's Response:
Our eyes are opened; forgive us God

One: forgive us, but do not let us rest

The People's Response:
Our eyes are opened; forgive us God

One: forgive us, but do not let us be idolatrous

The People's Response:
Our eyes are opened; forgive us God

One: forgive us, God of Shalom, forgive us

ALL: Our eyes are opened; forgive us God

(Valerie Bridgeman Davis)

Prayers for Illumination

God, in Christ Jesus, you appeared to your disciples after the resurrection—behind closed doors, needing a word from you. Speak peace to us, now, and let us hear your voice in the proclamation of your truth. Help our doubt in this hour, even as you extend proof of your presence—scarred hands and a healing heart. Amen.

(Valerie Bridgeman Davis, Second Sunday of Easter, Year A)

Lord, like the disciples walking to Emmaus, we often fail to recognize you. Open our eyes to see you today. Open our ears to hear what you are saying to us today. Lord, as you did with those walking to Emmaus, spend time with us in fellowship until our hearts burn. Speak a divine message through a human vessel today. Amen.

(Kwasi I. Kena, Third Sunday of Easter, Year A)

(Matthew 10:24-25)

Lord, as we prepare to receive your Word, help us, like students, to humble ourselves before you, our Teacher.

Help us to surrender our hearts to you, so that we might take this Word and live by it as you, our Teacher and Master, have so graciously showed us.
In Jesus' name, we pray. Amen.

(Joseph W. Daniels, Jr., Fifth Sunday after Pentecost, Year A)

(Psalm 13)

Lord, open our eyes to see your grace afresh today. Open our ears, to hear your mercy anew today. We've been suffering for a long time, God, and we need to hear a word from you. We've been a long time in our family dysfunction. We've been a long time in our relationship folly. We've been a long time in poverty and economic pain. We have been too long in sin and shame. Lord, give light to our eyes today and encouragement to our souls, so that our hearts can rejoice in your salvation. Elevate our hopes because of the positive expectations we have in you. Speak Lord, we pray, in Jesus' name. Amen.

(Joseph W. Daniels, Jr., Sixth Sunday after Pentecost, Year A)

Giving

We live, God gives! Hallelujah!
We cry; God supplies! Hallelujah!
We need; God speeds! Hallelujah!
So let us with joy, joy, joy
Return what God has given.

(Ciona D. Rouse, Second Sunday in Advent, Year A)

Call to Giving

(Based on Psalm 95)

God is a great God above all gods. God is greater than our problems and God's
hand reaches to the depths and the heights, the sea and dry land. Come, let us
worship the rock of our salvation with our giving; come into God's presence with
our song, our thanksgiving, and the gifts of our lives and our substance. God is our
God and we are the people of God's pasture, and the sheep of God's hand. Give.
Give. Give.

(Valerie Bridgeman Davis, Third Sunday in Lent, Year A)

Dear friends, let us be like Abraham who stepped out in faith and gave God his all. Hoping against hope, this old, childless man continued on the path to the Promised Land, believing that God would make good on the promise of causing him to be "the father of many nations." We can look through history to see so many who gave against all hope: Harriet Tubman, who gave over and over again to provide freedom for the enslaved; Mary McLeod Bethune, who started a school with just $1.50; Martin Luther King, Jr., who gave the money from his Nobel Peace Prize and even his life to a Civil Rights Movement, trusting that God would give the increase. Indeed, God does give the increase to whatever we give. And so now at this time, let us give of our substance, even as we give our whole selves into the ministry of our Lord.

(Marilyn E. Thornton, Third Sunday after Pentecost, Year A)

Lord, as we come now to this time of giving, we invite those gathered here today to remember just how generous you've been to us:
You are the God who provided a job when we had none,
education when we couldn't pay for one,
family and fellowship when we were lost and done,
Peace of mind when we couldn't find any,
hope when the naysayers around us were plenty.

Lord, you've been good to us. You keep giving us the best that you've got. Freely, we have received from you. Empower us now to give freely, to support your work. In the name of the One whose gift to us is without a price tag, Jesus the Christ. Amen.

(Joseph W. Daniels, Jr., Fourth Sunday after Pentecost, Year A)

(Based on 1 Thessalonians 1:1-10)

Your ministry, and that of this congregation, makes a difference in the lives of people throughout the world. Like the church in Thessalonica, 'your faith, love and steadfast hope in Christ' will be remembered. Worship God now with your tithes and offerings, so that others can experience God's love, hope and liberation.

(Lillian C. Smith, Twenty-second Sunday after Pentecost, Year A,)

You don't have to give,
but you keep giving.
You don't have to love,
but you keep loving.
You don't owe us anything,
but you give us everything.
Thank you for these gifts we return to you.
Use them for your justice and righteousness! Amen!

(Ciona D. Rouse, Second Sunday in Advent, Year A)

Lord, each day that you wore human flesh, you gave lovingly–without reserve. Today, let us follow your great example. Receive our expressions of love: our finances, our love of God and neighbor, our service and our prayers. Amen.

(Kwasi I. Kena, The First Sunday after Christmas, Year A)

Offertory Prayer

Dear God, we thank you for the privilege of giving to you, who has given us everything. Bless these gifts of love. Increase them and increase your spirit in us that we may be as willing servants as Abraham, Harriet, Mary, and Martin, so that our community will grow in the knowledge and love of your kingdom. In Jesus' name, we pray. Amen.

(Marilyn E. Thornton, Third Sunday after Pentecost, Year A)

Lord, as we come now to this time of giving, we invite those gathered here today to remember just how generous you've been to us:
You are the God who provided a job when we had none,
education when we couldn't pay for one,
family and fellowship when we were lost and done,
Peace of mind when we couldn't find any,
hope when the naysayers around us were plenty.

Lord, you've been good to us. You keep giving us the best that you've got. Freely, we have received from you. Empower us now to give freely, to support your work. In the name of the One whose gift to us is without a price tag, Jesus the Christ. Amen.

(Joseph W. Daniels, Jr., Fourth Sunday after Pentecost, Year A)

Offertory Prayer
(Genesis 22:1-14)

Lord God, as we approach this offertory moment, may our giving reflect how grateful we are to you for providing a ram from the thicket–from moment to moment and generation to generation. Just as you provided for Abraham, you continue to provide for us. We are reminded that you have provided for us in our deepest trials and greatest tests. We are reminded that you provided for us through the terror and suffering of the Middle Passage. We are reminded that you provided for us amid the choking thorns of Jim Crow and discrimination. We are reminded that you have provided a way for us through immigration proceedings and green card worries. We are reminded that you have provided that check when we didn't know where the money was coming from, that job when all other employers said, "no." We're reminded that you have been our God through family strife, community disenfranchisement, cultural chaos, depression, and despair. We are reminded that because you have provided, our tests have become testimonies; for you have strengthened us, blessed us, and prospered us for your purposes. Lord, you have been good to us. Now as we come before you this day with a fresh chance to give, may our material gifts reflect gracious and giving hearts for the rams that you have provided from moment to moment and generation to generation. You are worthy to be praised–in Jesus' name. Amen.

(Joseph W. Daniels, Jr., Sixth Sunday after Pentecost, Year A)

Call to Discipleship

People of God, hear and obey the gospel proclamation. In the midst of being tested and humbled, cling to that which is real. Hear the moans of the weak, and the wailing of the sick and diseased. Listen to scriptures and songs; hear God calling you through them. See the evil and injustice that surrounds us. Soften your heart to react with love. Rejoice and be filled with the goodness of the Lord.

(Carolyn W. Dandridge and Catrinia N. Harrison, First Sunday in Lent, Year A)

Call to Discipleship
(Based on 1 Peter 1:3-9)

We have an opportunity. Let's not miss it. We are called into a living hope through the resurrection of Jesus the Christ. We are called into an imperishable, undefiled, unfading inheritance. Even as you face trials, you are enabled to do so because of Christ's glorious and indescribable joy. Friends, renew your commitment to receive the outcome of faith, that is the salvation of your soul.

(Valerie Bridgeman Davis, Second Sunday of Easter, Year A)

Invitation to Baptism

At his baptism, God anointed Jesus with the Holy Spirit and with power and Jesus went about doing good and healing all who were oppressed by the devil. The Apostle Peter preached peace by Jesus and the message spread throughout Judea, beginning in Galilee after Jesus was baptized. There is cause to celebrate–God shows no partiality. Whether rich or poor, educated or uneducated, God's love extends to all. The simple message that Jesus Christ died for our sins so that we might have new life has been told around the world for centuries.

Giving your life to Christ remains relevant because people continue to search for life in all of the wrong places. Who needs peace today? Who needs a touch from the Lord today? Come now and receive new life through Jesus Christ. If you want to be baptized today, on the day that we celebrate the Lord's Baptism–come now.

(Kwasi I. Kena, Baptism of the Lord, Year A)

Communion

Invitation

Jesus has invited everybody to dine at the table. Everything here is free!
Free from the bondage of sin to a life of peace. Everything here is free!

(Tim Warner, General Use, Year A)

Closing Communion Prayer

Unison

We gathered today as the body of Christ and sat at your table. We dined on a feast of the bread of life and a never drying fountain. Some came in humility, while others were broken. Some communed without realizing your glory, while others stood on the mountaintop praising your name. As we leave this place, O God, go before us. Enable us to reflect Jesus and his teachings in all that we say and do. As we take these blessed loaves of bread to the needy, be in the midst of the fellowship. Let this bread be a testimony of your greatness and of our remembrance of you until the next time we gather at your table in the name of Jesus, shalom and amen.

(Carolyn W. Dandridge and Catrinia N. Harrison, Transfiguration Sunday, Year A)

Communion Prayer

Abba, Father, we approach your throne with a broken spirit and contrite heart,
thanking you for the freedom and opportunity to worship and praise you.
We thank you for your unswerving grace and mercy.
Cleanse our hearts, and renew a steadfast spirit within us.
Help us to walk in love, as Christ also has loved us and given himself for us.
Holy Spirit, teach us to have strong love for one another,
enabling us to effect change in the world.
Fill our hearts with patience, love, acceptance,
and understanding toward one another.
Teach us to let love be our greatest aim.
In Jesus' name, Amen.

(Toni Payne, General Use, Year A)

The Great Thanksgiving for Black History Month
(Adapted from A Service of Word and Table II)

The Lord be with you.
And also with you.

Lift up your hearts.
We lift them up to the Lord.

Let us give thanks to the Lord our God.
It is right to give our thanks and praise.

It is right, and a good and joyful thing,
   always and everywhere to give thanks to you,
   Father Almighty, creator of heaven and earth.

You formed us in your image
and breathed into us the breath of life.
When human cruelty reared its ugly head,
you sustained your people
and made it possible for us to survive
the middle passage,
auction blocks,
whipping posts

and forced labor.
You softened the hearts of many
who worked in secret on our behalf
You lifted our heads with the message
that God sides with the oppressed
and delivers the captives.
You strengthened our hands
to struggle for justice and freedom.

And so,
　　with your people on earth
　　and all the company of heaven
　　we praise your name and join their unending hymn:

Holy, holy, holy Lord, God of power and might,
Heaven and earth are full of your glory.
Hosanna in the highest.
Blessed is he who comes in the name of the Lord.
Hosanna in the highest.

Holy are you, and blessed is your Son Jesus Christ,
who left the comforts of glory
to live among a people estranged from God.
By his life and example he taught us
that it was possible to love our neighbors
and live together as family.

By the baptism of his suffering, death, and resurrection
　　you gave birth to your church,
　　delivered us from slavery to sin and death,
　　and made with us a new covenant
　　by water and the Spirit.

On the night in which he gave himself up for us,
　　he took bread, gave thanks to you, broke the bread,
　　gave it to his disciples, and said:
"Take, eat; this is my body which is given for you.
 Do this is remembrance of me."

When the supper was over, he took the cup,
　　gave thanks to you, gave it to his disciples, and said:
"Drink from this, all of you;

this is my blood of the new covenant,
    poured out for you and for many
    for the forgiveness of sins.
Do this, as often as you drink it,
    in remembrance of me."

And so,
in remembrance of these your mighty acts in Jesus Christ,
we offer ourselves in praise and thanksgiving
    as a holy and living sacrifice,
    in union with Christ's offering for us,
 as we proclaim the mystery of faith.

Christ has died; Christ is risen; Christ will come again.

Pour out your Holy Spirit on us gathered here,
    and on these gifts of bread and wine.
make them be for us the body and blood of Christ,
that we may be for the world the body of Christ,
    redeemed by his blood.

By your Spirit make us one with Christ,
    one with each other,
    and one in ministry to all the world,
until Christ comes in final victory
    and we feast at his heavenly banquet.

Through your Son Jesus Christ,
with the Holy Spirit in your holy church,
all honor and glory is yours, almighty Father,
now and forever.
Amen.[3]

---

[3] Great Thanksgiving for Black History Month: from Service of Word and Table II (c) 1972, 1980, 1985, 1989 by United Methodist Publishing House. Used by permission.

Creedal Statements

A Creed Inspired by the Beatitudes

I believe in the One who lifts my poor and broken spirit,
Restores my soul and gives me new life in God's kingdom on earth.

I believe in the One who puts love in my heart and
Gives me peace that overshadows all woes.

I believe in the One who nourishes our bodies and
Keeps our souls healthy with the Bread and Water of life.

I believe in the One who gives us mercy to give as a gift to others and
Appoints peacemakers in the midst of war.

I believe in the One who keeps me standing on holy ground
Though surrounded by false gods,
False teachings,
And false doctrines.

I believe in the One who kept
Moses and Miriam
Jacob and Rebecca
Paul and Priscilla and Aquila

Martin Luther King, Jr. and Rosa Parks
and Howard Thurman.
(*Additional names may be added, or the names may be changed to reflect other national, historical, or biblical witnesses*).

I believe in the One whose face we will see at the end of this journey in the fulfillment of God's kingdom

I believe in the awesome power of the Holy Spirit
I believe in Jesus
I believe in God.

(Carolyn W. Dandridge, Fourth Sunday after Epiphany, Year A)

A Statement of Faith for Black History Month

(For suggested use of this affirmation, see Black History Month Celebration *on page 221.)*

I believe in God, who formed people of every nation, tribe and language
and calls the whole earth to love and service
I believe this same God loves color and character; ethnicity and diversity
I believe in the God of Harriet Tubman
Frederick Douglas
Richard Allen
Jarena Lee
Paul Lawrence Dunbar
Mahalia Jackson
Martin Luther King, Jr.
Fannie Lou Hammer
(Insert the names of local and other heroes and sheroes of faith.)
And African American *(or African diasporan/African)* ancestors and believers who
paved the way in faith, leaning on the Lord
I believe in Jesus Christ, who came as an ethnic Jew
to call people of all races to Abba, parent of us all
I believe in the Spirit of God, who works in and through
the gifts of peoples of all races and tongues
and who infuses African Americans (or African diasporan/African) with prophetic
and anointed gifts for the whole church
I believe in the community of faith, from many grains, but now one loaf in solidarity
With God, Three-in-One, who stands with poor and disenfranchised people
throughout the world
I believe in God's promise to finally triumph over all evils, from racism to sexism,
global and local,
And who will establish a reign of justice and peace that will have no end.

(Valerie Bridgeman Davis)

An Affirmation of Faith for Trinity Sunday

(This affirmation may also be used for Pentecost Sunday.)

I believe in the Spirit of God
that swept over the face of the deep and created the heavens and the earth.
I believe this same Spirit swept over the waters of our Middle Passage and created
the will to live deep in the hearts of our African ancestors.
By God's Spirit did we come to know that we were created by God
and belonged to God, even in the days of chattel slavery.

I believe in the Spirit of God, the Almighty Creator.

I believe in the grace and love of the Lord Jesus Christ,
which has kept us as a people through racism, Jim Crow, lynchings, discrimination, disenfranchisement, and post-affirmative action.
I believe the same Jesus who suffered on the cross and who equipped
the apostles with grace in their persecution suffers with us in our tribulations and
provides grace for every situation.
I know that Jesus is walking with us even now and that God loves us no matter
the challenge.
I believe in the Spirit of the Lord Jesus Christ.

I believe in the Holy Spirit
and in the sweet communion of saints She creates.
I believe that by the Holy Spirit our ancestors were empowered to found Sunday
schools, churches, learning centers, and homes that have given us the foundation
for the abundant living that we have been promised.
By Holy Spirit we are empowered to live in community
with one another with love and peace
I believe in the power of the Holy Spirit.

I believe in Triune God,
who has covered our past, present, and future with grace, hope, and love.
May the grace of the Lord Jesus Christ, the love of God,
and the communion of the Holy Spirit be with us,
now, and forevermore. Amen.

(Marilyn E. Thornton, Trinity Sunday, Year A)

Affirmation
(Based on Matthew 14:22-33)

Jesus you walk toward us on our stormy lakes.
Even when we are terrified, you keep coming to us.
When we cry out in fear you say, "Take heart."
When we question you, you bid us, "Come to me."
When we start to sink, we can cry out, "Lord save me!"

When we need you, you say:
Take heart;
it is I.
Do not be afraid;
come to me.

(Tony Peterson, Twelfth Sunday after Pentecost, Year A)

An Affirmation

First Voice:
Who do people say that I am? (Matthew 16:13)

Second Voice:
Some say you are a figment of imagination.
Some say you are irrelevant.
Some say you never existed.
Some say your existence doesn't matter.
Some say you belong to another race.
Some say you belong to another party.
Some say you belong to the status quo.
Some say you are weak.
Some say you look after the rich, the powerful, and the famous.

First Voice:
Who do **you** say that I am? (Matthew 16:15)

(Invite responses, and then end with the following.)
You are our Lord
You are our Teacher
our example

our Savior
our friend
our comforter
our advocate
our companion.
You are mother and father when none can be found.
You are love!

You are the firstborn of all creation.
You are for all races and peoples.
You belong to no political party.
You are on the side of the poor and weak.
Your arm is long and bends toward justice.

You are our source and our destination,
Our Alpha and Omega,
Our beginning and end.
You are the Christ, the Son of the living God.

(Tony Peterson, Fourteenth Sunday after Pentecost, Year A)

This World Is Not Our Home
A Creedal Statement

I believe
This world is not our home,
We are passing through as pilgrims
and ambassadors of a heavenly city.

I believe that in that heavenly city
all pain and suffering will be taken up in Jesus
We will thirst no more
Nor hunger anymore,
For we will feast at the welcome table
And the leaves of the trees will heal the nations

I believe we will celebrate God
when we cross over Jordan in death to live forever
We will sing, dance, and shout
with angels and ancestors for all time.

(Written in a group at the 2004 gathering of 21st Century Africana Worship)

The Strange Fruit that Saved You and Me

A Creedal Statement

We believe in Jesus, the center of our joy,
from whom comes all that is good and perfect.
He walked through every set
as he hung out with pimps, players and power brokers.
He was lynched on a tree,
the strange fruit that saved you and me.
He got up with all power in his hands.
He is the man with the master plan,
with us in our darkest hour.
He is the lover of my soul,
my friend when I have no friend.
Right now he is hanging with the One
who makes a way out of no way.
He protects me and provides for me.
He is a fence around me everyday.
He watches over my comings, my goings,
in the alley, in the schoolyard, in the back stairwells.
He's my RIP for eternity.

(Written in a group at the 2004 gathering of 21st Century Africana Worship)

We believe God sits high and looks low
We believe God stepped out on nothing and hung the moon and stars in the sky
We believe God's got the whole world in his hands
We believe God delivered the children of Israel
We believe god delivered the Hebrew boys from the fiery furnace
We believe God delivered Daniel from the lion's den
And God will deliver us
We believe God can make a way out of no way
We believe God is able to do anything but fail
We believe God is good all the time and all the time, God is good
We believe that we cannot beat God's giving
We believe in the God who gave Jesus
We believe

We believe

We believe in the Spirit of the Living God
Giver of peace when the storms of life are raging
We believe the Sweet, Sweet Spirit is the active Presence of God
and Jesus Christ, filling us with Love, compassion and praise.
We believe that the Spirit of the Living God grants us courage
We believe
We believe

We believe the church is a community of saints and sinners
Who gather in love to worship God
We believe, in this community, called into being by Christ
We learn about God's call and the responsibilities of discipleship.
We believe the fellowship of believers will witness
God's unconditional love to everyone
We believe
We believe

(Written in a group at the 2004 gathering of 21st Century Africana Worship)

Benedictions/Sending Forth

(Based on Psalm 118:24; John 10:10)

Today is the best day of your life.
It is the only day you have to live.
Yesterday is history; tomorrow may never be history.
Live this day to the fullest–encountering God, enjoying God;
blessing God by blessing and being blessed by God's people.
And may the grace of God: loving us before we knew we were loved;
the grace of God: sustaining us in the chaos and calamity surrounding us;
the grace of God: already present in the days yet to come;
the grace of God whose favor knows no end:
Uphold you, uplift you, and embellish you in ways that bring the world joy.
In the name of Jesus we pray. Amen.

(Joseph W. Daniels, Jr., General Use, Year A)

Closing Blessing

Praise be to the God and Father of our Lord Jesus Christ, the Father of compassion and the God of all comfort, who comforts us in all our troubles, so that we can comfort those in any trouble with the comfort we ourselves have received from God. (2 Corinthians 1:3-4)

(Junius Dotson, Fourth Sunday in Lent, Year A)

Sending Forth

The Scriptures say that we need more than bread for our lives; we must feed on every word of God. Go, feast on the words of the Most High, Creator God. Be overwhelmed by God's goodness and let your life be your praise, until we meet again. Amen.

(Carolyn W. Dandridge and Catrinia N. Harrison, First Sunday in Lent, Year A)

Benediction
(Based on Psalm 16)

God is our protection; the One who has given us pleasant places and a broad space on which to stand; we have a goodly heritage. Go forth in the knowledge that God is faithful along the path of life; Go forth knowing that you are in the presence of God's full joy and that at God's right hand are your pleasures forevermore. Go in peace to serve the Lord!

(Valerie Bridgeman Davis, Second Sunday of Easter, Year A)

(Based on Romans 5:1-8)

Now unto him, who died for the ungodly, while we were powerless; whose love for us knows no boundaries and has no end; to Jesus the Christ, be glory, majesty, dominion and power, now and forevermore. Amen.

(Joseph W. Daniels, Jr., Fourth Sunday after Pentecost, Year A)

Benediction
(Adapted from Jude 24-25)

Now to the One who is able to keep you from stumbling,
And to present you faultless before the presence of
His glory with exceeding joy,
To God our Savior, who alone is wise,
be glory and majesty, dominion and power,
Both now and forever. Amen.

(Eugene Blair, Seventeenth Sunday after Pentecost, Year A)

Benediction

Saints of the Lord, it is time to go down from this mountaintop of worship.
Go now and live everyday like it is your last.
Leave this place and look forward to your "well done, good servant."
At a moments notice, be ready to pray, praise, and shout!

In all things, glorify God through the Savior, Jesus Christ. Amen.

(Eugene Blair, Eighteenth Sunday after Pentecost, Year A)

Benediction

Go forth with the authority Christ gives to his church.
Cry out against wrong.
Heal where there is hurt.
Feed, clothe, and defend those who live on the margins.
Train up children in the ways of God.
Show no contempt for youth; comfort the elderly.
In all things, give God the glory and praise, now and forever. Amen.

(Eugene Blair, Nineteenth Sunday after Pentecost, Year A)

Dismissal

You have been called and invited to experience God's abundant feast. The invitation to experience God's kingdom, now, is yours. Accept the invitation and live. Go forth in love. Go forth in peace. And may God's peace and love go with you. Amen.

(Lillian C. Smith, Twenty-First Sunday after Pentecost, Year A)

Dismissal

Beloved of God, we have experienced God's glory today. Just as God has been with us in the past, God will go with us when we leave this place. Go forth in peace! Go forth in love! Go forth in hope!

(Lillian C. Smith, Twenty-second Sunday after Pentecost, Year A)

Resources for Special Days

Women's Day

Litany of Honor for Women Here and around the World

L: With holy reverence, we remember irreplaceable women, O God. We honor those who nurtured us and taught us to honor and love you, O God.
P: May their example of Christian faith help transform us into your image.

L: We honor women who feed the hungry, clothe the unclothed, befriend the lonely, and comfort the comfortless. We bless them for unselfishly loving your people as you love us.
P: May you continue to meet their needs as they minister to others.

L: We honor women grieving the loss of loved ones.
P: May You, O God, continue to comfort them with your Word, spoken and blessed. May we learn to encourage them as they have encouraged us.

L: We honor women pregnant with your unborn sons and daughters, O God.
P: May you shelter them and the children they bear under the shadow of your almighty presence.

L: We honor our sisters throughout the world who need your spiritual, economic and physical healing.

P: May you meet their needs, Holy One, according to your riches in glory, we pray.

L: We honor all the women who have gone before us, named and unnamed.
P: We give you thank, O God.

L: We bless those who wept for us, rejoiced with us, wiped out tears, prayed for us, and laughed with us.
P: We give you thanks, O God.

L: We bless those who undauntedly sacrificed for us.
P: We give you thanks, O God.

L: We honor all those who stand alongside and for these women. We bless those who encourage them to dream, who bring out the best in them, who help them bear their burdens, and who love them rightly, O God.

All: May you watch over and keep all your people, these women and all who love them, with your care, gracious God. Consecrate this day for your glory. In the name of the Triune God, the one who parents us and creates us, who redeems us, and empowers us forever. Amen.

(Stacey Cole Wilson)

Men's Day

Litany for Men's Day

[In memory of Joseph T. Thornton (1923 -2005),
who loved his wife and raised his children and held on as long as he
could.]

All: How good and pleasant it is when the brothahs live together in unity.

Leader: For the brothahs who love their wives and raise their children
    For the brothahs who dwell in the house of the Lord;
    Let our community be a source of strength as they hold on.

All: How good and pleasant it is when the brothahs live together in unity.

Leader: For the brothahs who stand on street corners or sleep in bus stations
    For the brothahs who live in libraries and have no place to call home.
    Let our community be a source of strength as they hold on.

All: How good and pleasant it is when the brothahs live together in unity.

Leader: For the brothahs who have PhD's
    For the brothahs who struggle and make only D's
    For the brothahs who drive BMW's
    For the brothahs who would like to be a BMW
    You know–a Black Man Working
    Let our community be a source of strength as they hold on.

All: How good and pleasant it is when the brothahs live together in unity.

Leader: For the brothahs who teach
    For the brothahs who preach
    For the brothahs who drink
    For the brothahs who think
    That there is nothing for them in this world or the next;
    For those who have hope and for those who are hopeless
    Let our community be a source of strength as they hold on.

All: How good and pleasant it is when the brothahs live together in unity.

Leader: Whether in the jailhouse or the schoolhouse
    In gangs or in covenant groups

Whether in health or sickness
In addiction or recovery
Let our community be a source of strength as they hold on.

All: How good and pleasant it is when the brothahs live together in unity. How good and pleasant it is when ALL the people live together in unity!!!

(Marilyn E. Thornton)

Mother's Day

Gathering Call

One: Somewhere this morning, mothers are awakening and saying: "Good morning, Lord. Thank you for another day!"

Many: Good morning, Lord. Thank you for another day!

One: Somewhere this morning, mothers are awakening and saying: "Oh Lord, not another day."

Many: Oh Lord, not another day.

One: Somewhere this morning, mothers are awakening and saying: "Oh Lord, order my steps this day."

Many: Oh Lord, order my steps this day.

One: Somewhere this morning, mothers are awakening and saying: "Oh Lord, will I make it through this day?"

Many: Oh Lord, will I make it through this day?

Leader: Somewhere this morning, mothers are awakening on the other side of glory and saying: "Oh Lord, we knew you didn't bring us this far to leave us. Thank you, Lord, for eternal life!"

All: Oh Lord we know you didn't bring us this far to leave us. Thank you, Lord, for eternal life!

Opening Special Music

(Could also be danced, using "My Lord, What a Morning," "I Don't Feel No ways Tired" or "Give Me Jesus".)

Morning Prayer

Oh Lord, thank you for waking us up this morning to pay homage to you through your son, Jesus Christ. We pay homage also this day to our mothers, whether we knew them or not. We pay homage to our mothers, whether they showed us love or not. We pay homage to them Lord, because you chose women to usher new life into the world. Through their pains, we have been born onto this earth. We love them just because they are our mothers. Through the pain of Jesus, we have been born again on earth and in heaven.

Thank you for mothers everywhere. To mothers who are strong, grant gentleness and understanding. To mothers who are weak, grant grace sufficient to meet their every need. God of our mothers, hear their prayers and fill them with your Divine Spirit and Wisdom. "While on them you are calling," do not pass us by. Amen.

(Sherrie Dobbs Johnson, Mother's Day, Year A)

Mother's Day

Gathering Call

Leader:
God made Sunday for mothers.
A time to be "Mary's" and sit at the feet of Jesus.

People:
Come, mothers, lay your burdens down and sit at the feet of Jesus.
Come, fathers, lay your burdens down and sit at the feet of Jesus.
Come grandmothers and grandfathers,
lay your burdens down and sit at the feet of Jesus.
Come children, lay your burdens down
and sit at the feet of Jesus.
Come, singles, lay your burdens down
and sit at the feet of Jesus.
Come, neighbors, lay your burdens down
and sit at the feet of Jesus.
Come, strangers, lay your burdens down and sit at the feet of Jesus.

Leader:
Come, ye that love the Lord, and sit at the feet of Jesus.

Opening Hymn: "Marching to Zion" #3 *Songs of Zion* or #733 *The United Methodist Hymnal*

Opening Prayer

God, our protector, God, our defender, Father and Mother God, thank you for never leaving us alone. No matter who else lets us down, we know you never will. Although we may not understand when bad things happen to us, help us to call upon your name. No matter what we call you, you are the same God of Abraham and Sarah, of Isaac and Ishmael, and of Hagar. You are also our God. We know you more clearly through your Son, Jesus Christ. We know that you are the same

God who sent water to Hagar in Beer-Sheba and to Moses and the Hebrews in the wilderness. Send water now to the women, children and men in Iraq, and in Afghanistan, and in the United States, and in Israel, and in Haiti, and everywhere your children thirst, whether for water or for your Spirit.

If you save us, we will be saved indeed, on earth and in heaven. Thank you for helping us hold out just one more day. Thank you for hearing our cry. Thank you for answering our prayers in your time and in your way, and for giving us what we need, even before we knew we needed it.

You are, indeed, a great God, and so we give you praise. Mother God, this is your special day. Hear our praise as we celebrate it with you. Amen.

Scripture: Genesis 21:9-21

Special Music: "Sometimes I Feel Like a Motherless Child" #83 *Songs of Zion* (solo, instrumental or with dance)

Sermon Suggestion: "Mother's Helping Hand"

(Summary: Those who 'mother' need a helping hand from time to time. Many of us have been mothers who needed a helping hand, and God did not let us down. God sent us friends, helpmates, opportunities. Many of us are mothers in need of a helping hand right now. Our God can do exceedingly, abundantly more than we can ask or even imagine.)

Abraham and Sarah chose to be God's people, because they believed God had chosen them. Their Egyptian slave woman, Hagar, also had a relationship with the God of Abraham. God comforted Hagar when she ran away from home while she was pregnant with Ishmael. God was her helping hand. Sixteen years later, when Sarah's anger drove her away for good, God helped her keep her son from dying in the wilderness from thirst and starvation. God cared for Hagar in her wilderness experience just as God had provided food and drank to the Israelites in their wilderness wanderings. God made the descendants of Hagar's son a Great Nation, too, just as God made a Great Nation of Sarah's son.

Many mothers of African descent can identify with this biblical mother of African descent from Egypt. What God did for Hagar, God has done down through history and will continue to do for us.

Prayer: So, now, God of us all, teach us how to allow you to comfort and protect us as you comforted and protected Hagar. Help us turn away from doing harm for harm, evil for evil. Show us how to love all your children. Show us the way to be helping hands to all your children. We do not want to wait until we all get to heaven to sing together and shout together of your amazing love. Free us to shout now! Amen.

(Sherrie Dobbs Johnson, Mother's Day, Year A)

Father's Day

A Father's Day Call to Worship

One: In a day when so many men are absent, we cherish the love of our fathers.

Many: Thank God for fathers who comfort and encourage.

One: Thank God for fathers who build character and inspire us to greatness.

Many: Thank God for fathers who teach morality and model decency.

One: Thank God for fathers who lovingly convince boys to become men.

Many: Thank God for brave fathers who have the courage to resist being absent.

All: Lord, on this Father's Day, may we encourage more men in our community to pick up the mantle of fatherhood!

(Kwasi I. Kena, Father's Day, Year A)

Litany/Responsive Readings

I Love My Black Daddy!

One: I love my Black daddy!

Many: In the quietness of the noise that clamors to convince me that he and other Black men with children are nothing,

One: I love my Black daddy!

Many: In the rush of crescendos that resound to persuade me that he ain't done nothing, didn't do anything, ain't anything for me,

One: I love my Black daddy!

Many: With divine love, my Black daddy embraced my beautiful momma, committed his life to my beautiful momma. His energy, his investment. Shared his seed with my beautiful momma. And because of that, I'm here.

One: Do you love your Black daddy? I love my Black daddy!

Many: Against every societal odd, he made a way for his family.

One: I love my Black daddy.

Many: Working full-time, going to school full-time at the same time.

One: I love my Black daddy.

Many: Our future at the front of his mind. Options, opportunities, and possibilities he worked long and hard so that all of us might find.

One: I love my Black daddy.

Many: No matter what you say about him.

One: I love my Black daddy.

Many: Yes, he had his faults and failures, his sins and his shortcomings. But I got mine, don't you, too?

One: I love my Black daddy anyhow.

Many: Yes, he stumbled and fell short of the glory of God. I saw him do it

on several a times. Ain't proud of it, ain't happy about it, times where it made me mad and cry. But he's my daddy. With his trials, he's my daddy. With his tribulations, he's my daddy.

One: And yes, I'm going to love my Black daddy!

Many: So we rise on this Father's Day to say, I'm proud of my Black daddy! Proud of his strong stature. Proud of his spiritual strength. Proud of his angelic anointing. Proud of his divine demeanor. He ain't perfect, but he has earned my praise.

All: Thank you, God, for my Black daddy! Thank you, God, for my Black daddy. Thank you, God, for my Black daddy! Glory to your name, God. Amen!

(Joseph W. Daniels, Jr., Father's Day, Year A)

Get It Right with Daddy
(Based on Luke 15:18)

One: Let's pledge today to get it right with daddy.

Many: Father's Day, unlike Mother's Day, sometimes brings pain rather than joy. It causes me to remember anger and resentment when I was a girl, or a little boy.

One: Let's pledge today to get it right with daddy.

Many: I'm not going to fake it, honoring Dad may not be easy. Particularly if he caused mess in our lives. Particularly if it was sleazy.

One: I've got to pledge today to get it right with daddy.

Many: He may have cursed our mom, and abused our family. Left us hanging when we needed him, I don't understand it, for the very life of me.

One: But the answers can be found, when we get it right with daddy.

Many: He is one of two that God used to create you. One of two necessary for you to understand you. It's easy to dismiss him. Easy to despise him. But much of life can't go on, until you reconcile with him.

One: Let us pledge today to get it right with daddy.

Many: So let's rise and find him, get up and go to him, even if it hurts, even in our shame. Yes, get up and find him, go and track him down, even with our fears, and with our pain.

One: Deliverance will come when we get it right with daddy.

Many: He may be dead and gone, nowhere to be found. Through a few conversations, you may find him still hanging around. But whatever you must do to pick up his scent, be like the prodigal, he got up and went.

One: Pledge today to get it right with daddy.

Many: You might find some answers when you track him down.
      Some stuff might make sense on the road you journey down.
      Like the prodigal, there may be a feast waiting for you.
      Maybe like others, information leaving you kinda blue.
      But peace can be found only when you pursue that part of you.
      Your father on earth. Your Heavenly Father with the glue.
      For daddy may have failed, his life lost in the mix.
      But whatever he broke, our Heavenly Father can fix.

All: Pledge today, pledge today. Pledge today. To get it right with daddy!

(Joseph W. Daniels, Jr., Father's Day, Year A)

Pastor's Appreciation Sunday

Gathering Call

Leader: Blessed are those who mourn, for they shall be comforted.
People: Blessed are those who comfort, for they are a blessing.

Leader: We come into this house because of the
      times we have mourned and been comforted,
      times we have wandered and been guided,
      times we have doubted and been assured,
      times we have misbehaved and been loved.

Blessed are we who mourn, for we have been comforted.
People: Blessed are those who comfort, for they are a blessing.

Leader: Blessed are those who mourn, but can yet find time to comfort.
      Blessed is the one who knows the
      words to comfort,
      wisdom to guide,
      faith to assure,
      patience to love.

Blessed is our pastor. He/she is a blessing. (Name) has comforted us for (number) years. We thank You Lord for this special servant's gift of turning mourning into comfort! Today we honor our pastor, the one who's led us Sunday after Sunday in worshipping you Lord.

This Sunday we still gather to worship you, Lord, especially for sending us our pastor!
People: Blessed are those who comfort, for they are a blessing!

(Sherrie Dobbs Johnson)

Martin Luther King, Jr. Day

Introductory note: This worship service was celebrated on January 15, 2003, at the Wightman Chapel of the Scarritt-Bennett Center in Nashville, Tennessee. The Center for Worship Resourcing posts it here so that churches and communities who may want to adapt it for use in their settings will have the benefit of this powerful recollection of the voice of Dr. King.

Those born after 1968 did not hear the speeches of Dr. Martin Luther King, Jr., on the evening news; and many of us born before 1968 only recall them in the brief "sound bites" that are used in our yearly MLK celebrations. "The Making of a Prophet" provides an opportunity for both younger adults and older adults to hear and reflect upon several of the historic speeches that shook the foundations of America and forever changed how we live with one another. This service compares the experiences of Moses to those of Martin Luther King, Jr., and provides an opportunity for those present to reflect upon the ways that God prepares people to stand as prophets.

Planning Considerations

For this service, you will need:

• One or more skilled readers to be the "voice" or "presence" of Martin Luther King, Jr.
• One narrator
• Up to six readers, who will be seated at various places in the pews as part of the congregation
• One or more soloists
• One or more musicians on piano/organ and/or other instruments that are familiar to your congregation's worship life. (Note: Songs may be done without musical instruments, as was often the case during the Civil Rights Movement.) (optional)
• Candles or tea lights to be lit in memory of those who suffered or died during the Civil Rights Era. (optional)
• Colorful banners with headlines from the Civil Rights Era (optional)

Meditation

> We hold these truths to be self-evident, that all men
> are created equal, that they are endowed by their
> Creator with certain inalienable rights, that among
> these are Life, Liberty, and the pursuit of Happiness.
> – *Declaration of Independence*, Thomas Jefferson, 1776

It would take nearly two centuries for these words to become a reality for all Americans–due in large part to Dr. Martin Luther King, Jr., a man who allowed God to make him a prophet. But what is involved in the making of a prophet? How do we know if it is our turn to stand up for a righteous cause? What responsibility do we have when God reveals to us that we can no longer ignore injustice? What is the price of answering God's call to be prophetic? The lives of Moses and Martin may help us discover answers to these questions. Perhaps today you will hear God's call to stand as prophet, to speak and to serve.

Prelude, Welcome, Procession

"Go Down, Moses" (UMH 448)
(Congregation sings while seated.)
Procession may include readers, narrators, community/church officials, singers, banners, and so forth.

God Notices Suffering People

Scripture (read by narrator)
Exodus 2:23-25

Martin's Childhood Reflections

Martin's childhood reflections reveal his struggle with racism at an early age. Suggested reflections, delivered in the first person, may be adapted from Martin and Malcolm and America: A Dream or a Nightmare, *by James Cone (Maryknoll, NY: Orbis Books, 1991), Chapter 1, "The Making of a Dreamer (1929-55)," pages 19-57. See especially page 23.*

Historic Events from the Civil Rights Era

Readers share headlines from the Civil Rights Era while seated among worshipers in the congregation. For larger sanctuaries, consider the use of a cordless microphone.

Reader 1:
Brown vs. Board of Education: U.S. Supreme Court Bans Segregation in Public Schools

Reader 2:
"Segregation now, segregation tomorrow, and segregation forever." George Wallace Stirs Crowd in His Inaugural Speech as Governor

Reader 3:
Fourteen-Year-Old Black Youth, Emmet Till, Brutally Lynched

Reflections from Martin's High School Years

Reflections from Martin's high school years reveal that Martin, like other African Americans living in the South, was forced to deal with segregation laws and the feelings of second-class citizenship that these laws created. Suggested reflections, delivered in the first person, may be adapted from Martin and Malcolm and America: A Dream or a Nightmare, *by James Cone (Maryknoll, NY: Orbis Books, 1991), Chapter 1, "The Making of a Dreamer (1929-55)," pages 19-57. See especially page 25.*

More Historic Headlines From the Civil Rights Era

Reader 4:
Eugene "Bull" Connor Leads Officers in Mass Arrests. Hundreds of Protestors Viciously Clubbed and Savagely Attacked by Police Dogs.

Reader 5:
Four Young Black Girls Attending Sunday School Die in Bombing of the Sixteenth Street Baptist Church.

Congregational Response
"Go Down, Moses" (refrain only)

God Prepares a Deliverer

Scripture (read by narrator)
Exodus 3:4-10

Martin's Reflections on Church and Morehouse College

By the time that Martin entered Morehouse College, he had begun to actively resist the bitterness that the experience of racism in childhood and youth could easily have created. He learned that a significant number of whites also felt that racism and segregation were wrong. Suggested reflections, delivered in the first person, may be adapted from Martin and Malcolm and America: A Dream or a Nightmare, *by James Cone (Maryknoll, NY: Orbis Books, 1991), Chapter 1, "The Making of a Dreamer (1929-55)," pages 19-57. See especially pages 25 and 26.*

More Events from the Civil Rights Era

Reader 6: Black and White Freedom Riders Board Buses to Test Desegregation Laws

Reader 1: Mob of 200 Stones and Firebombs Bus Carrying Freedom Riders

Martin's Call to Ministry

Suggested reflections, delivered in the first person, may be adapted from Martin and Malcolm and America: A Dream or a Nightmare, *by James Cone (Maryknoll, NY: Orbis Books, 1991), Chapter 1, "The Making of a Dreamer (1929-55)," pages 19-57. See especially pages 26 and 27.*

Historic Event Draws King into Civil Rights

Reader 2: Fifteen-Year-Old Claudette Colvin, High School Student, Pulled From Bus, Handcuffed, and Taken to Jail for Refusing to Give Up Her Seat to A White Passenger.

Martin Struggles with Personal Involvement in Civil Rights

What should I do? I have a wife and a young family. The dangers of speaking out against racism are real and often end tragically. This is my first pastorate in a silk-stocking Baptist church that caters to black middle-class values. What will they think if I come in and develop a reputation as a rabble-rouser? The members of Dexter Avenue are the black bourgeois who believe that black people can make it if they "study hard, work hard, save their money and stay out of trouble."

Additional reflections, delivered in the first person, may be adapted from Martin and Malcolm and America: A Dream or a Nightmare, *by James Cone (Maryknoll, NY: Orbis Books, 1991), Chapter 1, "The Making of a Dreamer (1929-55)," pages 19-57. See especially pages 35 and 36.*

Narrator:
But life is not convenient. Trouble never knocks before bursting into the room. The time for Martin to decide was at hand. This was a time for seeking God's guidance.

Congregational Response
"Lead Me, Guide Me" (TFWS 2214) (This may be sung by a soloist or by the congregation.)

Historic Turning Point

Reader 3:
Rosa Parks Arrested for Refusing to Give Up Her Seat to a White Passenger.

Martin and Rosa Parks

The incident involving Rosa Parks was no accident. She was tracked down by God's loving purpose in the struggle for righteousness.
Additional reflections, delivered in the first person, may be adapted from Martin and

Malcolm and America: A Dream or a Nightmare, *by James Cone (Maryknoll, NY: Orbis Books, 1991), "We Must Love Our White Brothers," pages 120-150. See especially page 134.*

The Prophet Faces the Mixed Reactions of the People

Scripture (read by narrator)
Exodus 6:6-9

Martin shares insights about the opposition he faced among different factions of his people.

The African American community approached the Civil Rights Movement and its struggle for equality with mixed feelings. Many instinctively knew that power concedes nothing without a struggle – a struggle that would eventually cost many their lives and their jobs.

Consider using excerpts where Martin challenges black leadership in "Give Us the Ballot," Address Delivered at the Prayer Pilgrimage for Freedom 17 May 1957, Washington, D.C. This speech may be found at mlkonline.net.

Soloist
"Ain't Gonna Let Nobody Turn Me Round"

It is reported that Ralph Abernathy, a prominent leader of the Civil Rights Movement, taught this song to a mass meeting of the black community held in Albany, GA, in the summer of 1962. It was televised by CBS and soon became identified with the Civil Rights Movement. It can be found in Jerry Silverman's Songs of Protest and Civil Rights *(New York: Chelsea House, 1992), pages 56-57.*

The Prophet Courageously Confronts Pharaoh

Scripture (read by narrator)
Exodus 7:14-16, 20

Martin Openly Confronts Racism in the United States

Consider using excerpts from "Letter from a Birmingham Jail," which appeared in King's book Why We Can't Wait, *1964. This speech may also be found at mlkonline.net.*

Responsive Reading
Psalm 13 (UMH 746)

Martin's Response

Consider using excerpts from Dr. King's Montgomery Alabama Address: "How Long? Not Long?" given 25 March 1965 at the end of the Selma-to-Montgomery march, steps of the capitol, "Message Delivered at the Prayer Pilgrimage." Excerpts of this speech may be found in James Cone's Martin and Malcolm and America: A Dream or a Nightmare *(Maryknoll, NY: Orbis Books, 1991), Chapter 8, "Shattered Dreams (1965-68)," pages 213-243. See especially page 219.*

Narrator: Many people may have preferred Dr. King to limit his outcry to the realm of racial equality and civil rights. But the call of a prophet is to speak against injustice anywhere, even in times of war.

Modern Headlines
(Consider using headlines from recent news.)

Martin Shares His Reflections about Vietnam

Consider using excerpts from Martin's speech Beyond Vietnam, *delivered April 4, 1967, in New York, N.Y.*

Narrator: If Dr. King were alive today, it is certain that he would raise challenging moral questions for our nation to consider. But his voice was silenced on April 4, 1968, when a sniper's bullet assassinated Martin Luther King, Jr. on a hotel balcony in Memphis.

Congregational Response
"O Healing River"
by Fran Minkoff and Fred Hellerman Copyright information for this powerful hymn may be found at
http://www.gbod.org/worship/default.asp?act=reader&item_id=3863&loc_id=17, 19.

Candle Lighting and Remembrance

Worshipers are invited to come to the altar or a separate table and light a candle or tea light in memory of those who suffered or died during the Civil Rights Movement.

Call to Prayer
"Lord, Listen to Your Children Praying" (TFWS 2193) *(This may be sung during the candle lighting or after the candles have been lit in silence.)*

Hymn of Praise
"Lift Every Voice and Sing" (UMH 519)

Sending Forth

Suggested sending forth: When Elijah fled to Horeb after his confrontation with the 450 prophets of Baal, he complained to God that he alone was the only faithful prophet yet living (1 Kings 19:14). God responded that there were thousands of faithful people remaining in Israel. As we contemplate the empty place that Martin Luther King, Jr.'s death has created, we are forced to consider that the next great prophets may already be in our midst. Today's sending forth comes in the form of a question: Is it you? Is it you? Is it you?

Service Notes

This worship service was celebrated on January 15, 2003 at the Wightman Chapel of the Scarritt-Bennett Center, in Nashville, Tennessee. It was designed by the following people:

> Kwasi I. Kena, Director of Evangelism Ministries, GBOD, The United Methodist Church

> Safiyah Fosua, Director of Invitational Preaching Ministries, GBOD, The United Methodist Church

> Tom Albin, Dean of the Upper Room Chapel, The Upper Room, The United Methodist Church

> Becky Waldrop, Program Department, Scarritt-Bennett Center, Nashville, Tennessee.

Black History Month Celebration

Introit

"I Love the Lord", *(sung by psalmist)*

Call to Worship

One: The God who loves us calls us to worship
Many: We love the God of all creation and gladly we come

Songs of Welcome and Praise

"Welcome into this Place" #114 African American
Heritage Hymnal (AAHH)

"Amen, Siakudumisa " (Xhosa melody, South Africa)
122 (AAHH)

Litany of Affirmation *(based on Psalm 124)*

One: If the LORD had not been on our side–
Many: Let all the people say, if the LORD had not been on our side

One: If the LORD had not been on our side–let Israel say–
Many: If the LORD had not been on our side when we were attacked, when anger flared like a flash fire against us.

One: If the LORD had not been on our side, our enemies would have swallowed us alive.
Many: Our ancestors would have all perished in the Middle Passage.

One: Our ancestors would have all died in slavery in the Americas
Many: If the LORD had not been on our side–let all the people say–if the Lord had not been on our side, the flood would have engulfed us.

One: If the LORD had not been with us, the torrent would have swept us into the seas; the raging waters would have swept us away.
Many: Praise the LORD who has not let us be torn by their teeth.

One: Praise the LORD, we have escaped like a bird out of the fowler's snare.
Many: Praise the LORD, the snare has been broken, and we have escaped.

One: Our help is in the name of the LORD, the maker of heaven and earth.
Many: God is our help, the maker of heaven and earth.

ALL: Our help is in the name of the LORD, the maker of heaven and earth.

Prayer of Confession *(unison)*

Stony the road we have walked and yet we forget our footsteps. We have too often not honored the faith of our foreparents. We have too often strayed from the righteous path. We have too often been drunk on the wine of the world, and not lived out the radical gospel of service and peace. We have too often lived in division and sin. Forgive us, O God. Call us back to our heritage; back to you.

Assurance of Pardon

Christ is our peace, and has torn down every barrier between us and heaven; between us and all humanity. He has broken down these barriers that separate by his life and has built us up into one body in God by the Spirit. Whoever repents and believes, he has promised reconciliation and peace. Let us live as people reconciled. Amen

Pass Signs of Peace and Reconciliation

One: Since we have been reconciled let us share the peace that has been given us in grace. May the peace of God be with you
Many: And also with you

Music: "I Need You to Survive" by Hezekiah Walker

Special Music

The Word Spoken

Affirmation of Faith *(unison)*

(In response to the challenge and encouragement we have received, let us stand and declare what we most surely believe

I believe in God, who formed people of every nation, tribe and language
and calls the whole earth to love and service
I believe this same God loves color and character; ethnicity and diversity
I believe in the God of Harriet Tubman
Frederick Douglas
Richard Allen
Jarena Lee
Paul Lawrence Dunbar
Mahalia Jackson

Martin Luther King, Jr.
Fannie Lou Hammer

(Insert the names of local and other heroes and sheroes of faith)

And African American (or African diasporan/African) ancestors and believers who paved the way in faith, leaning on the Lord

I believe in Jesus Christ, who came as an ethnic Jew
to call people of all races to Abba, parent of us all.

I believe in the Spirit of God, who works in and through
the gifts of peoples of all races and tongues
and who infuses African Americans (or African diasporan/African) with prophetic and anointed gifts for the whole church

I believe in the community of faith, from many grains, but now one loaf in solidarity
with God, Three-in-One, who stands with poor and disenfranchised people throughout the world.

I believe in God's promise to finally triumph over all evils, from racism to sexism, global and local, and who will establish a reign of justice and peace that will have no end.

Prayers for the People

Music: "Thank you, Lord"
(Please continue to hum as the intercessor lifts our burdens before God.)

Benediction

(Valerie Bridgeman Davis)

Ash Wednesday

Prior to Ash Wednesday invite members of your congregation to select a prayer partner for the Lenten season.

Opening Declaration

We come together to begin the Lenten journey. We confess our transgressions and open our hearts to receive the mercy and loving kindness of God, made available to us through the suffering and victory of the resurrected Lamb. We are the people of Yahweh gathered tonight [today] to be marked by the ashes of burnt palms.

Prayer of Confession *(based on Psalm 51)*

Invite each person to select one prayer partner. Decide which person will be Partner A and which will be Partner B as the congregation shares the following prayer of confession:

ALL: Have mercy upon us, O God. Our sins are always before us. We have sinned against you only, O God! You know the evil within each of us.

Partner A: Sin took control whenever "I" became more important than you.

Partner B: When you offered truth, I refused it and opened the door that leads to death.

ALL: Have mercy upon us, O God.

Partner A: In word or deed I have sinned by neglecting your teachings and requirements.

Partner B: I was born into sin, but do not wish to remain there forever. Only you, God, can recreate a clean heart in me.

All: Blot out our transgressions and cleanse us from all unworthiness.

Partner A: Lead me on the path of righteousness.

Partner B: Fill me with your eternal Spirit and never leave me alone.

ALL: Thank you for cleansing us. Thank you for erasing my sin from your memory. As we minister to the world, deliver us from guilt and shame. Let the world hear us sing songs of thanksgiving and praise. Free us to shout Hallelujah as our shattered spirits receive new life. Restore unto us the joy of your salvation. Restore unto us the joy of your salvation. Amen! Amen! Amen!

Sending Forth

Return to the world as ambassadors of Christ, living lives that please God. Begin and end your Lenten journey with love and patience. Remain confident of the sovereignty of our Lord Jesus the Christ. Be filled with the Spirit of God as you go in peace. Amen.

(Carolyn W. Dandridge, Year A)

Palm Sunday

Praise on the Streets

On this day, the whole city seemed to explode into praise on the streets while Jesus' enemies plotted his death in the shadows. As we celebrate Palm Sunday we are reminded that not everyone rejoices to see truth ride unhindered through the streets. There will always be someone or something opposing the righteous. But we are also encouraged to look past the gloom and doom of Good Friday to the sure coming of the Resurrection. So, on this day of celebration rejoice while you are able, 'cause trouble don't last always.

(Safiyah Fosua, Palm Sunday, Year A)

Ride On!
(Call to Worship Based on Zechariah 9)

Rejoice greatly, O daughter Zion! Shout aloud, O daughter Jerusalem! Look, your king comes to you (Zechariah 9:9a NRSV).
Ride on, King Jesus, no one can hinder you!

Look, your king comes to you; triumphant and victorious is he, humble and riding on a donkey, on a colt, the foal of a donkey (Zechariah 9:9b NRSV).
Ride on, King Jesus, no one can hinder you!

See the crowd coming into the city! Join the glad procession with songs of praise.
Ride on, King Jesus, no one can hinder you!

We come, lifting our palm branches shouting, "Hosanna to the Son of David! Blessed is the one who comes in the name of the Lord! Hosanna in the highest heaven!" (Matthew 21:9b NRSV).
Ride on, King Jesus, no one can hinder you!

On this holy day, we come with lifted hands, waving palms, and raised voices to proclaim that you are the King of Kings and the Lords of Lords!
Ride on, King Jesus, no one can hinder you!

(Followed by singing the Traditional Version of "Ride On, King Jesus" #77 Songs of Zion)

(Safiyah Fosua, Palm Sunday, Year A)

Triumphal Entry

Today, God, we rejoice with Christians everywhere that there was at least one day when Jesus received the recognition he deserved. We rejoice, knowing that his triumphal entry means that truth cannot remain hidden and that good hearts everywhere recognize truth when it appears. We stand in hope with people on many continents, in many circumstances who are waiting for the day when their truth can be told. We stand with them in faith knowing that the same God who could have commanded the rocks to shout truth in Jerusalem will not allow truth to be suppressed and good people to be crushed forever. Amen.

(Safiyah Fosua, Palm Sunday, Year A)

Gathering Words

We sing Hosanna! Throughout the world people of God gather with branches in our hands. We gather singing Hosanna! Blessed is the One who comes in the name of the Lord! Hosanna in the highest! Blessed be God forever and forever! Let us worship God.

(Valerie Bridgeman Davis, Palm Sunday, Year A)

Call to Worship

One: O Magnify the Lord with me, and let us exalt God's name together!
Many: We enter in, singing and dancing, with palm branches in our hands!

(Alternate Call to Worship based on Psalm 118)

One: O, Give thanks to the Lord who is GOOD!!!
Many: God's steadfast love lasts forever
One: O, Give thanks to God at all times
Many: God's mercy is everlasting
All: O, Give thanks, for God is good, God is good!

(Valerie Bridgeman Davis, Palm Sunday, Year A)

Invocation

No one but you, our God, can mend our hearts and strengthen our resolve. No one but you can help us see your salvation. Come, Holy One! Come, Hope of Zion!   Come, receive our worship! Come! Hear our prayers! Come! Answer and save! Come! We are waiting! Come! Hear our hearts' cries! Come! We are ready! Come! We are waiting! Come!

(Valerie Bridgeman Davis, Palm Sunday, Year A)

Our Times Are in Your Hands

(A choral reading based on Psalm 31:9-16)

Psalm 31:9-16 is part of the Liturgy of the Passion for Palm Sunday. This Choral Reading would also be appropriate for use at other services during Holy Week. Requires at least six readers.

Readers 1 and 2: Do you see that? Do you see trouble in the world?

Reader 3: My eyes grow weak from seeing the trouble in the world.

Readers 3 and 4: My eyes grow weak with sorry; my soul and my body with grief.

Reader 2 and 4: I'm tired of looking at death, disease, destruction.

Reader 5: I'm weary of groaning, being consumed with anguish.

Readers 1 and 6: Do you see that? Do you see the trouble in the world?

All: Lord, have mercy, crucifixion on the way!

Reader 2: I'm tired of being weak, of my strength failing.

Reader 4: I'm tired of being afraid of my neighbors.

Reader 5: My bones are weak.

All: Do you think Jesus felt this way: weak, tired, weary?

Readers 4, 5, and 6: In the face of distress, people who did not believe?

Readers 1, 2, and 3: In a world full of sorrow?

All: Lord, have mercy, what distress!

Reader 1: Do you think people run from Jesus, too?

All: WHAT!!!!! *(Repeated over and over by all readers, some on top of other voices.)*

Reader 1: Shattered legacy; world so full of terror on every side . . .

Readers 1 and 2: Do you see that?

Reader 3 and 4: Can you trust in God?

Reader 5: What, and say, "You are my God?"
All: Yes, and say, "You are my God!" How else do you face the uncertainty?

Reader 3: How else do you face the uncertainty? How else?
All: Oh, God! Our times are in your hands; our times are in your hands
(Repeat several times.)

Reader 6: Deliver us and let your face shine on your servants
All: Are we the servants? *(Repeat several times.)* **Let your face shine on us!**
Servants?

Readers 1 and 2: Let your face shine on us servants.
All: Save us with your love that never fails.

Readers 5 and 6: Never fails! Love! In distress
All: Love! Never failing love! Lord, have mercy: Love! *(Repeat several times*
over voices, each, some together, some staggered.)

(Valerie Bridgeman Davis, Palm Sunday, Year A)

God's Loving Mercy Endures Forever

(Litany Based on Psalm 118:1-6)

All: Give thanks to the Lord, for God is good; God's love endures forever.
One Voice: Let the people of God say: His love endures forever.

Many Voices: Let the priests who serve in prayer say: His mercy endures
forever.
One Voice: Let all who reverence the Creating God say: His love endures forever!

All: We know what it is to cry out in anguish and fear.
One Voice: God's love endures forever.

All: God is with us; we will not be afraid.
One Voice: Let all who reverence the Saving God say: His love endures forever!

All: The Lord is our help and refuge; God's love endures forever.
One Voice: We put our hope in God rather than governments.

All: God's love endures forever!

(Valerie Bridgeman Davis, Palm Sunday, Year A)

Enter In and Shout About It

(Litany Based on Psalm 118:19-29)

One: Open the gates of righteousness.
Many: Enter in and give thanks to the Lord.

One: This is the gate of God.
Many: Enter in and be saved!

One: This is the gate of God.
Many: Give thanks as you enter in.

One: This is the place where God answers.
Many: Enter in; give thanks to the Lord for salvation!

One: The stone the builders rejected is the strongest part of God's house.
Many: Jesus is that stone; give thanks as you enter in.

One: The stone that was rejected is our Rock and strength.
Many: The Lord has made it so, and it is marvelous in our eyes.

One: This is the day the Lord has made.
Many: We rejoice, glad in it!

One: This is the day the Lord has made.
Many: We came to shout about it!

One: God is our salvation and our success.
Many: We came to shout about it!

One: Blessed is the One who comes in the name of God.
Many: We came to shout about it!

One: From God's sanctuary we bless you.

Many: We came to shout about it!

One: The Lord is God and shines on us.
Many: We came to shout about it!

One: With palm branches in hand and a song in our heart
Many: We came to shout about it!

One: We join the festive procession from age to age and place to place.
Many: Give thanks to the Lord, for God is good.

All: God's love endures forever. and we came to shout about it!

(Valerie Bridgeman Davis, Palm Sunday, Year A)

Good Friday

In the Name and Pain of the Crucified One

Faithful God, we stand in the dim shadows of a cross, longing for resurrection. But today we pause to remember the pain of the cross, and the pain of the crosses we've faced. We pause to cry for the Sudan, for Rwanda, for more than one-thirds of the African continent suffering from full-blown AIDS. As the disciples wept on that fateful day so long ago, we weep for the savior and for the tree, and all the trees that one represented, from which he hung. We cry for our ecology: birds slick from oil, forests decimated causing mudslides and runoff, air polluted from our disdain for the creation that cries with us. As those first disciples wondered whether that fateful day was the end of their dreams, we admit we are afraid that our dream of a just, nonviolent world is fleeting and in peril of death. Help us God as we live in the tension between this death and your seeming silence, the time after the crucifixion and before the resurrection—in the name and pain of the Crucified One, Amen.

(Valerie Bridgeman Davis, Good Friday, Year A)

What is Truth?
(A litany based on John 18:1-19:42)

One Voice: When Jesus finished praying in the garden, he went to meet his future—a certain death, a certain betrayal.
Many Voices: All around Jesus, people ask, "What is truth?"

One Voice: He was met by soldiers and false accusers.
Many Voices: All around Jesus, people ask, "What is truth?"

One Voice: Judas kissed away the meals and the miles they had shared together.
Many Voices: All around Jesus, people ask, "What is truth?"

One Voice: Peter tried to protect him from an inevitable and foretold end.
Many Voices: All around Jesus, people ask, "What is truth?"

One Voice: When he couldn't protect him, Peter's fear led him to deny him.
Many Voices: All around Jesus, people ask, "What is truth?"

One Voice: From hall to hall and heart to heart, they led him the dark of night to broken justice and false witnesses.
Many Voices: All around Jesus, people ask, "What is truth?"

One Voice: Pilate questioned his statement: "I came to testify to the truth," I came to be on the side of truth.
Many Voices: All around Jesus, people ask, "What is truth?"

One Voice: What was Pilate to do since he saw the truth with his eyes, but did not have courage to free it?
Many Voices: All around Jesus, people ask, "What is truth?"

One Voice: Crucify him still rings across time, because truth unrecognized always goes punished
Many Voices: And still we're asking, "What is truth?"

(Valerie Bridgeman Davis, Good Friday, Year A)

Easter Sunday

Call to Worship *(based on Acts 10:34-43)*

Come from every nation! See that God has pardoned! See that God shows no favoritism and accepts all who reverence God's name and do what is right! Come, God's witness to the world is risen indeed! Come! He lives! And everyone who believes in him will receive grace! Come, let's worship the Resurrected One!

Alternate Call to Worship *(based on Psalm 118: 1-2, 14-24)*

Come let's shout to God, for the victory over death is won! Hallelujah! The stone the builders rejected has become the steadying force in the building of God! The Lord has done this thing and it easy on our eyes! God made this day of salvation, and we're glad about it! Come, let us enter in and give thanks!

Prayer of Thanksgiving *(unison)*

How awesome are your ways, O God! With thanksgiving, we offer praise for the work you brought in Christ. In gladness we thank you for hiding us deeply into his sacred life. We bless you for raising us in and with Jesus Christ, giving us the power to proclaim with Mary Magdalene the Risen One, not only with our voices, but with our lives. In Jesus' name we pray, amen.

Litany *(based on John 20)*

Many: I have seen the Lord!

One: What was Mary to think when she saw the empty tomb? We would have been just as frightened, just as confused; how could she expect to proclaim:

Many: I have seen the Lord!

One: Yes, the disciples had been told to expect some radical oh-my-god-what-in-the-world-is-this happening, but an empty tomb? How could they expect to hear Mary proclaim:

Many: I have seen the Lord!

One: We would have run with Peter, skeptics that we are, eyes and hearts searching for a body instead of empty burial cloths. How could any of us expect to hear Mary proclaim:

Many: I have seen the Lord!

One: We would have cried, too, forlorn and feeling forsaken; we would not have known the familiar stranger asking us, "Why are you crying; who is it you are looking for?" How could Mary expect to proclaim:

Many: I have seen the Lord!

One: We would not have recognized his voice, or his body; we often don't recognize Him now in the world, so how do we expect to proclaim:

Many: I have seen the Lord!

One: But see! He goes before us, leading us into his world, up from the grave and bondage and invites us to proclaim:

Many: I have seen the Lord!

Offertory Prayer

Wonderful God: we come bringing ourselves as gifts in gratitude for the gift you gave in Christ Jesus, and for the gift he gave in his life and resurrection. These gifts of money represent for us our heart's thanks and our commitment to live as resurrection people. Amen.

Benediction

Go gladly into this world, raised with Christ, hearts lifted by his love. Live as though dead to all that keeps us from a life hidden with Christ in God. Amen

Alternative Benediction

Run with the news, my sisters and brothers! Run into a world that needs to know: Christ is risen indeed! Go, sure and filled with grace, knowing that you will see Christ again!

(Valerie Bridgeman Davis, Easter, Year A)

Pentecost Sunday, Year A

Call to Worship

One: Come! Let us bless the Lord who commands wind!

Many: Come! Let us worship the Three-in-One who appoints fire and flame as messengers!

All: Come! Let us bless our great and glorious Maker, giver of all good gifts!

Litany of Affirmation

One: God works in a variety of ways.
Many: But it is the same Spirit.

One: To one, God gives wisdom; to another a message of knowledge; to another, faith; to yet another, healing powers.
Many: But it is the same Spirit.

One: God gives miraculous powers, prophetic words and actions, discerning hearts, the power of languages, and the interpretation of those languages.
Many: But it is the same Spirit.

One: God works in a variety of ways, in marvelous ways.
Many: But it is the same Spirit.

Prayer of Confession *(unison)*

God of fire and wind, we confess we have missed the move of your Spirit in our lives and in your world. We have not been a Spirit-led church. We have not pursued your anointing or your sanctifying presence. We have not lived in holiness. Forgive us, we pray. Free us from bondage to life in the Spirit, through Jesus Christ our Lord. Amen.

Assurance of Pardon

One: Hear the good news! All who believe in Jesus Christ will have streams of living water flowing from within them, a stream of refreshing and of power. In Jesus Christ you are forgiven and empowered.

Many: In Jesus Christ, you are forgiven and empowered.

All: Hallelujah! Hallelujah! Hallelujah! Amen!

Prayer for Illumination *(unison)*

God of all power,
Open our ears, our eyes, and our hearts with a spirit of wisdom and revelation.
Help us to hear your voice, to see your ways, and to receive with joy your truth. In Jesus' name, amen.

(Valerie Bridgeman Davis, Day of Pentecost, Years A, B, C)

World Communion Sunday

Revised Common Lectionary Readings

Exodus 20: 1-4, 7-9, 12-20
Psalm 19
Philippians 3: 4b-14
Matthew 21: 33-46

Invitation

Brothers and Sisters, Christ has prepared the feast. At this table we join with people from around the world including Darfur, Port-au-Prince, D.C., Harlem and Rio. Christ invites to his table everyone who loves him, those who earnestly repent of their sin and seek to live in peace with one another.

Call to Confession

Saints, it is time to 'fess up. As good as we have tried to be, all of us have messed up this week and need God's forgiveness once again. Commandments have been broken right and left. We've lied. We've allowed jobs, money and people to exist as gods in place of God. The list could go on. Together, let us confess our sins before our loving God.

Prayer of Corporate Confession *(unison)*

God, we confess that although we knew better, we have sinned. We have not loved you or our neighbors the way we should. We have not always honored you with our time. We've coveted other peoples' stuff. And sometimes we have *called you out of your name.* Lord, forgive us. We apologize for the pain we've caused you. Forgive us of our sins and help us live in ways that give you joy–in Jesus' name, amen.

Words of Assurance:

Leader to people:

Brothers and sisters, there is good news today! God is faithful and just and has forgiven each of us for all of our mess. The thing you were embarrassed about – God has forgiven you. The thing no one else knows about, God has forgiven it! You have been given the graceful gift of another chance. Hallelujah! In the name of Jesus Christ, you are forgiven. Thank you God!

People to leader:

In the name of Jesus Christ, you are forgiven!

Leader and people:

Glory to God! Thank you Jesus! Amen.

The Great Thanksgiving

(Optional sentences for use with A Service of Word and Table II, pages 13-14 of The United Methodist Hymnal.*)*

Statements appropriate to the season or the occasion may be inserted where the asterisk (*) appears in the communion prayer.

*You sent your prophets to show your people the way.
When we disregarded them, you sent your son to save us from us.
You made the ultimate sacrifice for our reconciliation and redemption.

(Lillian C. Smith, Twentieth Sunday after Pentecost, Year A)

Post-Election Worship Service (November 2004)

Gathering Music
"God Is in Control" by James Hall and Worship & Praise

Gathering Call

Leader: Be in control, Lord, on this day after the Presidential Elections.

People: *(Sung to the tune of "Through it All" UMH #507)*

Be in control.
Be in control.
We've learned to trust in Jesus.
We've learned to trust in God.
Be in control.
Be in control.
Be in control of your world.

Leader: Some of us have come believing that the "true Christian," George W. Bush, has won, so we're jubilant. Some of us have come believing that the "true Christian," John Kerry, has lost, so we're crushed. Some of us have come not knowing what to believe, so we're confused. But, God, we've come tonight because no matter who is in the White House, you're in the Big House, so we give thanks!

People: *(Sung to the tune of "Through it All" UMH #507)*

Be in control.
Be in control.
We've learned to trust in Jesus.
We've learned to trust in God.
Be in control.
Be in control.
Be in control of your world.

Pastoral Prayer

Hymn of Invitation: "Kum Ba Yah" UMH #494

Scripture: Haggai 1:15b-2:5

Meditation: "Help *Is* on the Way!"

Presidential candidate John Kerry has said, "Help is, indeed, on the way," Our help comes from the Lord who made heaven and earth. That's the Good News.

The Bible text this evening is about a man, who also knew that "Help was on the way!" The prophet Haggai was commanded by God to tell Persian-appointed government officials what God wanted them to know and do.

The prophet Haggai was commanded to tell the returned and remnant people of Jerusalem, what God wanted them to know and to do.

They were commanded to build a new temple. The old one had been destroyed some 70 years earlier. And this temple was to be even more splendid than Solomon's temple. More splendid than Riverside Church. More splendid than the Crystal Cathedral or the National Cathedral in Washington. And with what? How could these poor people build a temple? So the people responded with that old familiar response, you know the one when we don't want to do something or think we can't do what we've been asked: "NOT YET."

But God was not discouraged; God's response to the people is found in Haggai 1:5b and following

> Consider how you've fared. You've sown much and harvested little; you eat, but you never have enough; you drink, but you never have your fill; you clothe yourselves; but no one is warm; and he who earns wages, earns them to put them into a hole.

> 'So do what I tell you. Start building. Go on, do this thing that pleases me. And guess what? I'll be with you. I, who made the stars of night, I who made the darkness bright. I will be with you.

God will be with *us*.

I've heard many this week say that their votes don't count. It doesn't matter what the citizens say or do, the government is going to do whatever it wants, they say. But we cannot become passive if we believe that God's work on earth is not finished. There's work enough for everyone. As the pastor of Riverside Church, Rev. James Forbes said to a discouraged group of people during the United Methodist General Conference, **"This is no time for foolishness!"** This is not the time to wait for someone else to do whatever needs doing. We are the ones call to work for justice and peace. We must work without ceasing, even as we pray without ceasing.

For the African slave in America, worship led to liberation. Their religion became their liberator. The slaves heard the Word of God and believed it. They believed that God was on their side, and spit out the bit about "servants be obedient to your masters." They heard far more than that. **They heard the bigger message**, that God loved all God's children and wanted them to be free and prosper. Most often the African slaves' temples were in swamps or in slave quarters or in the fields behind wet quilts to muffle their shouts and moans. They risked getting beaten with whips to worship. They risked their lives to worship. Worship was important to them because there they could have a special place to be in God's presence where they could release their misery, plan their deliverance, and thank God for just one more day. Help was on the way!

Many did not see freedom, but they knew it was coming. And it did.

[Offer your personal witness of how worship, work, faith, and the movement of the Holy Spirit contribute to building God's Kingdom on Earth.]

We as spiritual leaders have work to do. And God will be our helpmate.
Let us continue to **sing** songs of peace!
Let us continue to **fight** for the right!
Let us continue to **speak** truth to power!
Let us continue to **side** with the poor and oppressed!
Let us continue to **build** God's house into a place of spiritual splendor, courage and unity!

We may not know about tomorrow, but we know who holds our hand. Help *is* on the way. *Amen.*

Musical Response: "Here I Am, Lord" UMH #593

Dismissal with Blessing *(Unison)*

We go forth, trusting the Holy Spirit at work in us. And in the Spirit, we can do exceedingly, abundantly more than we can ask or even imagine! God is with us; we are not alone. Amen.

The Peace

(Sherrie Dobbs Johnson)

North American Prayer for the People of Sudan and the Continent of Africa

In our native land, they do not know peace, but peace knows them.
Grant them peace, Jesus, grant them peace.

In our native land, they trod a stony road, but a clearing is on the way.
Clear their paths, Jesus, clear their paths.

In our native land, conflict attacks hope before it is born, but hope can survive.
Give them hope, Jesus, give them hope.

In our native land, children walk a bloody road, but freedom is possible.
Grant them freedom, Jesus, grant them freedom.

In our native land, killing rings louder than singing, but faith promises a new voice.
Keep them singing, Jesus, keep them singing.

In our native land, people reach to us for help, but we often ignore their plight.
Help us listen, Jesus, help us listen.

We are extensions of your arms, and the traction of your feet.
We are the action to your prayers, and the voices to your song.

We stand in solidarity with our brothers and sisters across the sea.
We lift our voices for the voiceless,
praying for peace, for clarity, for hope, for freedom.
And, we lift our voices to sing a song for our native land,
for your proud creation, until victory is won.
Amen.

Sing the African American national anthem: "Lift Every Voice And Sing" (no. 519, *The United Methodist Hymnal*).

This prayer was written with the people of Sudan in mind but may be extended to include all of the troubled places on the continent of Africa.

(Ciona D. Rouse)

Deliverance

Opening Processional

The pastor and congregation enter the church from the outside and gather at the altar until after the Call to Worship.

The devotional leader sets the worship atmosphere by praying (perhaps with a prayer group) for the congregation to enter fully into worship and receive God's grace during the service.

Processional Song: "The Lord Is My Light," *African American Heritage Hymnal* #160

Altar Call *(The congregation is invited to the altar for a period of silence.)*

Call to Worship

Musician continues to play "The Lord Is My Light" softly during suggested reading. Voices may be combined to create a symphonic and/or choral effect for the opening call; or a single voice may read the opening call to worship.

Voice 1: Allow the spirit of the Lord to enter this house of worship.

Voice 2: Allow the spirit of the Lord to prepare your heart and mind for worship.

Voice 3: Think only of Jesus. Think of the beginning of his earthly ministry.

Voice 4: Consider the devotion of those who became his disciples.

Voice 5: Focus on the sacrificial death of Jesus.

Voice 6: Focus on the power the resurrection of Christ.

Leader: Open your hearts and let spirit of the Lord prepare you for worship.

**ALL: Lord, we are humbled by your spirit, which prepares us for worship.
We stand in awe of your sacrificial life and death.
We stand in awe of all that you have done for us.
We will rejoice in the strength of the Lord, and be of good courage!**

Song

Litany: "Deliverance" (based on Psalm 86, NKJV)

To be read with Young Adults as the People and Youth as the Leader.

People: In my life I have seen great pain and sorrow.
When I met you I found hope for tomorrow.

Leader: Bow down your ear O Lord, Hear me: For I am poor and needy. (Psalm 86:1)

People: I don't want to lose what I have been trying to gain.
Lord you have become my "something to ease the pain."

Leader: Preserve my life, for I am holy; You are my God: Save your servant who trusts in You! (Psalm 86:2)

People: I ask for forgiveness though I know I don't deserve it.

A love story gone wrong, we can work to mend it.
Be merciful to me O Lord,
For I cry to You all day Long.

Leader: Rejoice the soul of your servant. Teach me your way O Lord; I will walk in Your truth. (Psalm 86:4a, 11)

People: I apologize for what I have done.
I hope that the last song wasn't sung.

Leader: For to You, O Lord I lift up my soul. For You, O Lord, are good, and ready to forgive. (Psalm 86:4b, 5a)

People: Trials and tribulations I am ready to tread through,
But only if I can accomplish that side by side with you.

Leader: Give ear, O Lord, to my prayer; and attend to the voice of my supplications. In the day of my trouble I will call upon You, for You will answer me. (Psalm 86:6-7)

People: I can beg and plead, and wish as I may;
I would give anything just to have your peace.

ALL: But You, O Lord, are a God full of compassion, and gracious, long-suffering and abundant in mercy and truth. Oh, turn to us, and have mercy upon us! Give Your strength to Your servants (Psalm 86:15-16a)**.**

Liturgical Dance: To "Alabaster Box," by CeCe Winans (*Alabaster Box*, 1999)

Anointing
Suggested Song: "The Lamb," African American Heritage Hymnal *#179*

Benediction

(Carolyn W. Dandridge and Catrinia Harrison)

Opening Sentences at the Beginning
of a Bridal Procession

"This day, queen of essence and daughter of divinity, you leave your house and your home to unite with your king, whom the King of Kings has placed in your life. This day you place yourself before him forever, for all the people to see. Let him in these moments and for an eternity, admire your beauty. Let him in these moments and forevermore, adore your Black beauty and desire your divine elegance. As you are led to your king, decked out in the finest fabric framed for a queen, may you walk with joy and process with gladness as you rejoice in the goodness of the Lord.

And O king, as you witness God's beauty for your life come to take your hand, may your marriage be fruitful. May your children rise to be African princes and princesses. May they bless the earth, and may you and your house be celebrated throughout all generations. May your witness be praised by people now and forevermore. Amen!"

(Joseph W. Daniels, Jr.)

Index of Scripture

How to Use the CD-ROM

1. Place *The Africana Worship Book* CD-ROM in your computer's CD-ROM drive.

2. Go to My Computer and double click on the file named Africana_Worship_Book.pdf

3. The file will open in Adobe Reader ©, if you have this application installed on your computer. If you need to install Adobe Reader ©, you may download a free copy at www.adobe.com.

4. After opening Africana_Worship_Book.pdf, you may use the selection tool in Adobe Reader © to copy excerpts. You may then paste the selected material in your word processing application for use in worship settings.